May 10, 1998

To Avery + Beverly —

thanks for your support in easy times and hard —

Daniel P. [illegible]

TRANSFORMING HEALTH CARE

Action Strategies for Health Care Leaders

DANIEL J. ANDERSON

JOHN W. MORAN

BAIRD K. BRIGHTMAN

BARRY S. SCHEUR

AHA press

American Hospital Publishing, Inc.
An American Hospital Association Company
CHICAGO

This publication is designed to provide accurate and authoritative information in regard to the subject matter covered. It is sold with the understanding that neither the author nor the publisher is engaged in rendering legal, accounting, or other professional service. If legal advice or other expert assistance is required, the services of a competent professional should be sought.

The views expressed in this publication are strictly those of the authors and do not necessarily represent official positions of the American Hospital Association.

AHA is a service mark of the American Hospital Association used under license by American Hospital Publishing, Inc.

Cover design by Tim Kaage

ISBN 1-55648-232-9

Item Number: 108102

Dedication

To Alison and Terry, who know why more than words can ever tell

—D. J. A.

To Norma and Julian, for something to say and the means to say it

—B. K. B.

To Claudette and Wally, for their support and inspiration

—J. W. M.

Contents

About the Authors *vii*

Preface *ix*

Acknowledgments *xv*

CHAPTER 1

Market Leadership: What You Need to Know and Do 1

CHAPTER 2

Design Architecture: Symptoms and Prescriptions for the Healing Enterprise 13

CHAPTER 3

Core Process Redesign (CPR): Aligning Process with Strategy and Results 43

CHAPTER 4

Changing Health Care: You Must Try, Try, and Try . . . 57

CHAPTER 5

Enhancing Performance: Reinventing Management to Sustain the Gains 69

CHAPTER 6
Health Work: Maintaining Professional Balance and Effectiveness 85

Epilogue: Not *Just* Another Business *95*
Bibliography *103*
Index *107*

About the Authors

Dan Anderson, PsyD, is the founder and president of Changing Healthcare, Inc., a health care firm dedicated to the delivery of world-class consulting, coaching, and organizational design in the service of patients, professionals, and performance. A psychologist by training and business consultant by experience, Dr. Anderson has dedicated much of the last 20 years to the design and implementation of effective change strategies in hospitals, group practices, and managed care organizations in the United States, Europe, and Asia. He has served on the faculties of Harvard Medical School and Boston University's School of Medicine. Dr. Anderson also relies on his experience consulting to telecommunications, defense, technology, and transportation industry leaders to support his conviction that health care can never become just another business.

Baird Brightman, PhD, is a partner with Changing Healthcare, Inc., helping health practitioners and leaders to improve their professional effectiveness for competitive advantage. As he moved into leadership positions at some of the nation's leading health care institutions and assumed management responsibility for program staffs and budgets, Baird became interested in how people did their work—for better and worse. Impressed that very bright people often failed to meet critical work and business challenges, he developed structured assessment and development programs that allow individuals and work teams to rapidly diagnose and overcome the major obstacles to professional effectiveness. Dr. Brightman holds a master of science degree in assessment and applied research, a PhD in clinical psychology, and has served for 20 years on the faculty of Harvard Medical School.

John W. Moran, PhD, is a partner and chief operating officer of Changing Healthcare, Inc., helping clients with strategy, process management, executive team building, and organization redesign. He has consulted with medical product companies, pharmaceutical firms, hospitals, insurers, and medical groups in the United States, Asia, and Europe. He is the author of *Breakthrough Thinking* (1993), *Future Focused Organization* (1995), and *The Quality Function Deployment Handbook* (1998). He is a member of the Malcolm Baldrige Board of Examiners, a health care judge for the *USA Today* Quality Cup, a fellow of the American Society for Quality, an American Society for Quality certified quality manager, and a certified management consultant. He is chair-elect of the Quality Management Division of the American Society for Quality. He served on the faculty of the University of Massachusetts at Lowell in the Graduate School of Engineering for 20 years. Previously John worked for Polaroid Corporation in a variety of senior management positions in manufacturing, engineering, and quality.

Barry S. Scheur, JD, is the founder and president of the Scheur Management Group, Inc., a health care management and consulting firm in Newton, Massachusetts, specializing in the conceptualization and implementation of innovative and effective managed care solutions. He writes and lectures extensively on both the operational and futuristic trend in the provision of health care, as well as on innovative marketing strategies, the vital importance of customer service, and the newest challenges in the Medicaid and Medicare arenas. A graduate of Tufts University and Yale Law School, his advice and counsel have been sought by hundreds of HMOs, physician groups, insurance companies, and major employers—all of whom are trying to figure out how to make the health care system work from the perspectives of both quality and financial success.

Changing Healthcare, Inc., is a health care firm dedicated to the delivery of world-class consulting, coaching, and organizational design in the service of patients, professionals, and performance. Partners of Changing Healthcare provide strategy implementation consulting and facilitation to hospitals and health systems. The name reflects our vision, mission, values, and strategic intent. Our executive workshops and on-site consulting reflect the areas of expertise outlined in each chapter of *Transforming Health Care: Action Strategies for Health Care Leaders.* Changing Healthcare works with clients to enable accurate assessment of their culture's readiness for change, targets key areas for redesign, builds individual and team competencies to lead change, and applies health care–specific redesign tools to achieve the clinical outcomes and business results needed in the changing health care environment.

Preface

PATIENT CARE AND BUSINESS PERFORMANCE

Health care is not—and can never be—just another business. Healing can never be just another enterprise. In the last decade, however, health care organizations have confronted the need to achieve business results like any other business. Almost endless support from employers, insurance companies, and the government was the constant reservoir of fiscal vitality until the mid-1980s. The health care industry—hospitals, doctors, payers, pharmaceutical firms, and malpractice lawyers—drank at the golden trough of infinite reimbursement for costs plus margin. As with the defense and banking industries, most health care organizations' bottom lines got better and better as costs escalated.

No more. Humana, Incorporated, left the hospital business because it was losing money. Columbia/HCA, the largest health care organization in the world, was accused of gross fraudulence in optimizing Medicare reimbursement. Kaiser Permanente—one of the oldest and largest health maintenance organizations in the United States—is struggling to sustain its social mission and still be truly competitive. The federal government has cut its funds for postgraduate medical education at academic medical centers. A rush to merge, acquire, and squeeze independent health care organizations into fully integrated health care systems has achieved few of the intended savings needed to meet the loss of revenue. For many health care organizations—especially on each coast—the golden trough has gone dry. Just as the banking and defense industries have learned, health care organizations must also adapt to the rules of an often brutal business environment—or die trying.

From Pennsylvania Avenue to Wall Street to Main Street, many politicians, pundits, and business professionals concur that it's about time for such business adaptation, no matter how brutal the learning curve may be. We spend more of our gross national product on the development and delivery of health care services than any other nation in history and, arguably, get less care for each health care dollar spent than citizens of many other industrialized nations.

In other industrialized countries, for instance, everyone has access to health care without regard to personal capacity to pay for services or insurance. This is not true in the United States. How long can this situation continue? When will patients really revolt and storm the growing barricades to good care at reasonable cost?

As Regina E. Herzlinger so superbly documents in her recent book *Market-Driven Health Care*, the patient revolution for greater access, increased freedom of choice, scheduling convenience, and flexible delivery systems is just beginning. Patients and payers expect more care for fewer dollars as the nonnegotiable pivot points around which every successful health care organization must spin. Only those organizations—and those leaders—that achieve the delicate, dynamic balance of patient care and business performance will transcend the fate of those who pretend that health care can be run as just another business. Because it can't. You—as a health care leader—and we—as consumers and patients to be—won't let this happen. So our model is about *what works* and *how to act* to enable you and your organization to gain balance and momentum.

Models are illustrations of theories and assumptions. The gyroscope is our model for understanding what works in your health care organization. And without a theory of what works, all action strategies are futile and doomed to random failure. The chaos of working without any conscious theory and expressed assumptions is all around us. So if you have a better model—built on better theories—of what works in your health care shop, stick with it.

Alas, books and models do not change behavior. You do (or don't)! Just as books won't change you, theories and models will not change your health care organization. Models promise diagnosis of what does not work, and you already know a lot about what does not work inside your healing enterprise. For the most part, health care leaders are wasting money on comprehensive diagnosis and neglecting implementation—action strategies—in their use of theories, models, and consultants. So much of our daily behavior is built on vague hypotheses or false assumptions about how to act (behavior) to drive what works (systems) to achieve strategy implementation (goals). The intent of our model—the gyroscope—is to challenge and focus your thinking about what works and how to act in your healing enterprise.

Ultimately, this book is about changing health care behavior. *Yours.*

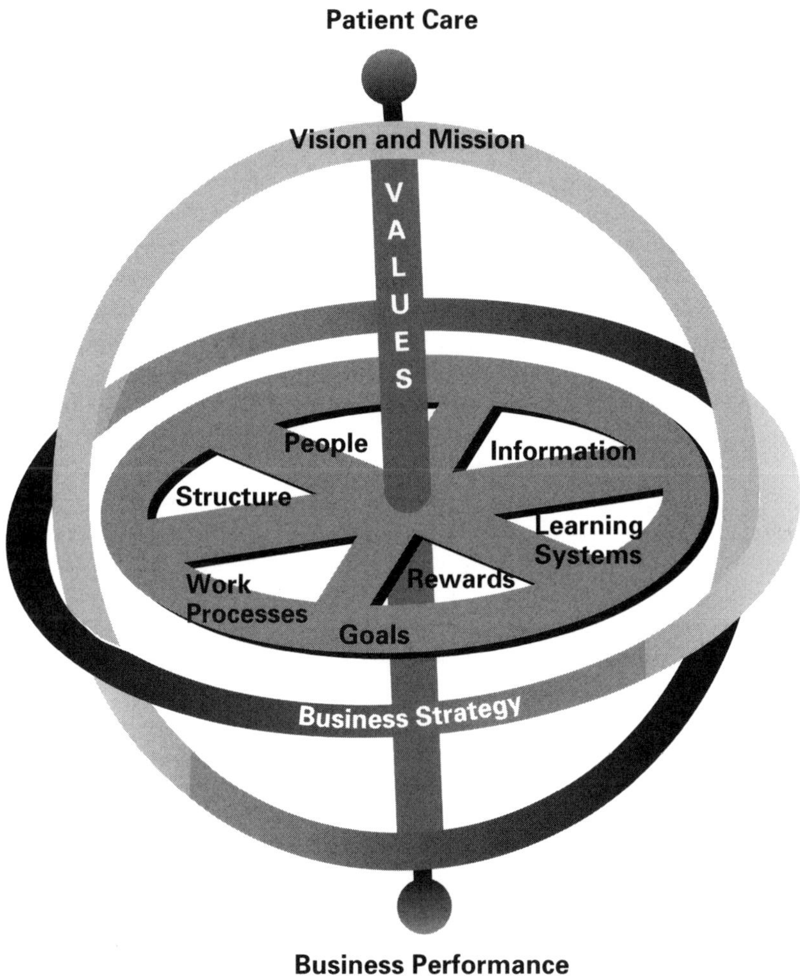

Adapted, with permission, from Laughing Bear Associates © 1997.

THEORY AND PRACTICE IN PARALLEL

If you are still hopeful that transformation is about *them*, you are not ready to read this book. This book is about changing the behavior of a particular leader of a health care organization. *You. Transforming Health Care: Action Strategies for Health Care Leaders* is really two books in parallel. The first book—let's call it *Transforming Health Care*—describes what works to enable health care organizations to deliver on their promise of excellence for both patients and performance. We have seen what works—and what doesn't work (again and again)—and will share a few critical lessons with you based on our experience. Our intent is to enable your health care organization to make critical leaps forward on the path to innovation, excellence, and effective implementation of key strategies for the next century. (Would you even consider reading a book that promised you less?)

The second book—let's call it *Action Strategies for Health Care Leaders*—is a user's guide for the specific behaviors that define how to act as a leader every day to assure dynamic alignment of what works—strategies, systems, structures—with how you act as a leader. Without this alignment of "what" and "how," your leadership will never achieve the results your patients and your market expect and demand. Our intent is to share examples and stories of how to act tomorrow to become a better leader for the next century. (Can you afford to stop reading this book?)

Chapter 1, Market Leadership, will take you on a guided tour of market strategies that identify future health care market needs and differentiate effective market solutions. It provides a path to critical orbits that your business strategy and strategic intent must achieve if your healing enterprise is to survive, compete, and successfully move into the next century. Without clarity of strategic intent, any further discussion of alignment is moot. Even with clarity, market leadership may smash itself on the shoals of mediocre implementation. We often ask health system leaders: "Would you prefer an A+ strategy with a B− implementation; or a B− strategy with an A+ implementation?" Chapter 1 concludes with an approach aimed at deploying your strategy for market leadership born of the lessons of the authors' century of experience consulting to health care organizations.

Chapter 2, Design Architecture, defines the critical design systems of the market-leading healing enterprise. The chapter identifies the symptoms of misalignment between strategy and organizational design that drive imbalance and slow momentum in most health care organizations today. Sample diagnostic questions provide health care leaders with the means for targeting areas requiring action strategies.

Chapter 3, Core Process Redesign (CPR), reviews strategies for dramatically improving work processes to improve both clinical outcomes and business results. This chapter defines action strategies for selecting the critical core processes, the right team leaders, and creating a charter for successful redesign. It shares the change technology, results achieved, and lessons learned through on-site design and implementation of (CPR) across several health care organizations.

Chapter 4, Changing Health Care, explores the skills that are at the heart of any effort to transform a teaching hospital into a learning health care system. The chapter focuses on the false assumptions and ineffective practices commonly encountered in many organizational change efforts. It discusses practical prescriptions for building effective, customized action strategies to sustain learning and a commitment to the constant changes in healing enterprises that market leadership will always demand.

Chapter 5, Enhancing Performance, defines an innovative, tested approach to managing performance in the recently redesigned health care organization. Those of you who walk the halls of health care as leaders in the redesigned organization must recognize that organizations—like individuals—suffer from what statisticians term regression toward the mean. In other words, just as most diets to design the body of our dreams (or youth) rarely survive into the new year, most redesigned organizations will rapidly return to previous misalignment without a systemic commitment to reward, confirm, and sustain new behaviors. And while the aligning of individual behavior with the new design may be painful, would you prefer the eternal diet of perpetual redesign? The true test of a redesign effort is whether people are motivated to confront and move beyond the all-too-human hunger for tradition, habit, and the more comfortable ways of "the good old days."

Chapter 6, Health Work, presents models and action strategies for nurturing and challenging people to be their best in a constantly changing workplace. Again and again we collectively bear witness to the brutal reengineering and "dumbsizing" of both health care and other industries. We simply cannot and will not afford a 70 percent failure rate for radical change efforts in health care organizations. Much of the failure of reengineering efforts results from how we care for the people who work in our organization. While a redesigned performance management is critical, no system can guarantee growth and excellence in a healing enterprise—only *people* can do that. This chapter provides the information, skills, and resources needed to sustain passionate commitment to professional collaboration, patient care, *and* business performance.

And finally, the epilogue returns to the question of which values form the axis of today's health care organizations and which values will be required to assure that health care never becomes just another business. This summary attempts to capture the voice of current health care leaders as they reflect on values in practice that drive their action strategies in the emerging world of changing health care.

Acknowledgments

There are more mentors, colleagues, students, and clients who have made the authors' experience and this book possible than can be named here. Nevertheless, a few deserve special recognition for whatever is truly good about this book. They include Rick Waks for his rigor and imagination in the development of our gyroscope model for design implementation and of the change technology at the foundation of core process redesign. Thanks, Rick. We also want to thank Jeffrey Mead for his contribution of knowledge and experience to our work on performance enhancement and Amy Avignon for her contribution to our work on change management. Thanks to Ken Lizotte of CareerScape for teaching us how to write a book proposal that might make it to market. Sunny Yando, PhD, a longtime mentor and friend, brought greater clarity to the complexity of the epilogue. Thanks, Sunny. Mason Singer (of Laughing Bear Associates) gives new meaning to the lyrics of an old Rod Stewart song—"every picture tells a story, don't it?"—with his genius in graphic design. And thanks to Judy Paavola, the office manager at Changing Healthcare, for gracefully ignoring political correctness and our occasional ill humor in getting this book to our publisher without driving them or us crazy.

And special thanks to our editor, Rick Hill, and all the folks at AHA Press for their constant support, gentle advice, and great good faith that *Transforming Health Care: Action Strategies for Health Care Leaders* could contribute to their vision of improving health through information.

While it seems best not to even begin mentioning clients or the specific health care leaders by name who contributed their wisdom and experience to each chapter and to the epilogue, we are indeed grateful to them. They are the source of our continued learning, professional development, and pleasure in work.

1

Market Leadership What You Need to Know and Do

THE HEALTH CARE MARKETPLACE AND MARKET DYNAMICS

Twenty years ago, the health care and insurance industries in the United States bore little resemblance to each other. You knew your health insurance had a deductible and coinsurance, but once you bought it, you knew that just about every health care service you needed would be paid for. There were no requirements for referral authorizations or designation of specific physicians as primary care providers, and you didn't see health insurers marketing their comparative benefits on television.

Fast forward to the end of this century. The five major insurance companies that historically dominated the indemnity insurance market—Travelers, CIGNA, Aetna, Metropolitan, and Prudential—are either radically different organizations or have disappeared entirely.

Traditional indemnity insurance has faded away like last year's second-place basketball team. Managed care advertising pervades the airwaves with claims for "personalized service," "more qualified doctors," and having "been credentialed as a company meeting rigorous regulatory standards for quality."

What happened here? If people liked their traditional way of getting health care services and paying for them separately with no linkage between those who deliver health care and its financing, then how come we are in the midst of such radical changes in the environment?

The answers may be found in two simple concepts:

1. Health care was thought of as practiced by doctors in their offices—doctors who made house calls when necessary and

who used hospitals as workshops. Hospitals were run as charitable organizations that provided high profiles for the community leaders and auxiliary volunteers who supported them.

2. Providing care was never conceived of as being a business. It was never a venture that needed to make a profit to satisfy shareholders or whose practitioners were concerned about big companies opening up competitive offices or hospitals down the street. You didn't see ads for "the business of caring," which has been a hallmark of CIGNA, a traditional insurance company that has moved into managed care both through development of its own plans and through its acquisition of Healthsource, a large, publicly held HMO company.

Change is inevitable in just about all sectors of the economy. But the transformation of health care from "seeing patients" to the business of managed care—combining insuring and delivering services to patients, the rise of for-profit medicine, and the selling of health care through consumer advertising—has left an industry in chaos and consumers yearning for the simpler times.

This book describes how organizations can work most effectively and humanistically to provide the kind of health care and payment services we want. While most people resist change in organizations and in their products, they learn to adapt because the new is always supposed to be better than the old. But amidst all this flurry of new health care businesses springing up at a prolific rate and of entrepreneurs figuring out unique ways to monitor and measure the quality and adequacy of health care delivery, there is still a small voice of the consumer and the caregiver asking: "What happened here?" and "How do we cope with this change?"

Our goal here is to set the stage for people to better understand the selling and packaging of the health care industry and what it portends for the future.

The phrase "managed care" has not been embraced altogether positively as exemplifying the best that our insurance and health care systems have to offer. There are very few health care executives, physicians, or corporate benefits managers that tout managed care as the most progressive and needed mechanism for treating sick people and paying for their care. Yet hundreds of millions of dollars have been directed toward the transformation of health care and insurance from a service to a business. Hundreds of millions of dollars have also been invested in start-up enterprises whose purpose is to service, improve, refine, or manage the care process, or to analyze the health care business data we have so suddenly become concerned about.

Is the new breed of health care delivery and insurance packaged as managed care to be applauded, reviled, or accepted? Will we get better service and more appropriate care, or will we simply get marketing and advertising pitches that promise us those things? The answers to some degree are still "blowing in the wind," but the trends that have shaped the packaging, promotion, and selling of health care give pretty good indicators of what the next decade will bring. It's not a bad picture, but it is a different one, and only time will tell whether the corporations that purchase health benefits and the consumers who pay for them and use them will put the brakes on the pace of change or accelerate it.

To understand today's health care environment and what it's like for the practitioners, professionals, and average citizens who make up its workforce, it's necessary to understand how business and marketing forces have come together to package not only what we now have, but what we will have in the future.

HEALTH CARE BUSINESS DYNAMICS

In the late 1970s, the concept of packaging and selling health care and insurance existed only in a few isolated markets with limited consumer appeal. Kaiser Permanente, the Group Health Association of Washington, D.C., and the Group Health Cooperative of Puget Sound were all examples of prepaid plans (to be known as HMOs) that integrated the benefits you received with the coverage you paid for. Initially, HMOs were facilities that employed doctors and provided more comprehensive care without the necessity of paying for deductibles and coinsurance. Care was prepaid in the sense that the premium paid every month was the amount you had to be prepared to lay out for health care.

The federal government passed the HMO Act in 1973 regulating these new start-up health delivery and financing organizations, but they were still relatively unaccepted in the marketplace. But one provision in the law provided that health plans approved by the government under specific circumstances could force large employers to offer their programs alongside the traditional indemnity insurance package. The HMOs had the advantages of comprehensive benefits and a fixed price, but with limited freedom to select doctors. People, especially people with families, became willing to accept the trade-offs of the first generation of HMOs.

The second generation of health plans came in the mid-1980s with the development of broader-based physician networks called independent practice associations (IPAs). These networks allowed for greater freedom of choice, as they were comprised of practicing doctors in the community who were willing to see HMO patients for the discounted fee-for-service reimbursement that the ever-growing number of health plans offered. Also in the mid-1980s, the government for the first time allowed Medicaid and Medicare beneficiaries to receive their services through HMOs. Some early abuses led to bankruptcies, poor quality, or, worse yet, nonexistent care. This occurred because a few quick-buck and fly-by-night artists recognized that, even with limited networks, paying for care up front with cash and then regulating the care that got provided afterward could be highly lucrative.

What the IPA did for a number of consumers was give them a way to get a bargain on their insurance with a reasonable trade-off in access. More important, however, people began to understand that the packaging and selling of health care as a product was a pretty good deal for people who needed low-cost, coordinated, and reliable care.

The third business wave took place in the late 1980s and early 1990s. A number of companies, some already in the hospital business and some started by entrepreneurs and physicians, discovered there were significant profit margins available by signing up large numbers of people for this insurance/delivery combination. Profits from these companies were very attractive in terms of operating publicly held companies with high earnings-per-share multiples. By the end of 1992, there were 24 national, regional, and local public companies selling HMO and managed care products. Travelers, Prudential, and the other insurance giants, not to mention Blue Cross organizations across the country, looked at this growth and saw opportunity to mimic those businesses. So managed care as a more restrictive and less costly alternative to indemnity insurance was born.

But people still didn't like the notion of having to get care approved in advance or being limited to a certain group of specific physicians or hospitals.

CRITICAL MISTAKES AND MISCALCULATIONS IN HEALTH CARE ORGANIZATIONS

The transformation in the organizational, operational, and financial components of health care delivery and insurance has left many managers, boards of directors, and even investment analysts wondering just what separates those that excel from those that cling precipitously to life. Repetition of key critical path errors in judgment or process constantly cripple or retard the future of many health care systems, institutions, and companies.

Change always takes place faster than we think possible, particularly when we try to deny the reality of its impending onset. But the evidence is all too apparent and happening all too often in health care. Consider the following:

- Two companies that didn't exist 15 years ago (PhyCor and MedPartners), in a field that didn't exist as a business 10 years ago (practice management), entered into a transaction in which PhyCor acquired MedPartners for $8 billion.
- The major health insurance companies whose names we would have associated with permanence and stability have gone out of the health care business, changed themselves through the acquisition of new companies, or face financial crises that never could have been contemplated for them. The Travelers' red umbrella no longer protects its customers from a rainy day. The Metropolitan Life Insurance Company disappeared from the health care scene. Many Blue Cross and Blue Shield plans face uncertainty. Aetna transformed itself into U.S. Healthcare, and CIGNA tried to seize the managed care marketplace through the acquisition of Healthsource. The Prudential Insurance Company, known as the Rock to millions of customers for decades, has radically changed its organization and its leadership in an effort to make headway against the advancing tide of the new wave of managed care companies.
- Large community hospitals and academic medical centers around the country are forming alliances and consolidating with their historic competitors in an effort to optimize efficiencies and exert leverage against these evolving large insurers and managed care companies.
- The Medicaid and Medicare government programs are being handled by for-profit managed care companies that compete for their enrollees against a backdrop of declining payments and budget crunching.
- Physicians, who for years have felt preyed upon by the transformation of health care delivery into balance sheets and profit and loss statements, are now organizing themselves to compete with insurers and control their destiny.
- The American health care system, which has always been perceived as providing the best care available in the world, is under assault by patients resenting and fearing the overriding constraints of business decisions that restrict access choices for care and impose restrictions on choices of physicians and hospitals.

In summary, the speed and degree of change has been truly revolutionary. Representatives of management, fiduciaries, and caregivers face decisions for which their training and experience have not prepared them. "Caring, while coping" is the challenge faced by individuals and institutions. Meeting this challenge is complicated by health care institutions and physicians that cannot make a correct diagnosis of their current condition and decide upon a remedy.

The pitfalls described below are ones that, once identified and classified, can be avoided by the institutions and caregivers that we have historically depended upon for the treatment of illness and disease.

Pitfall 1: Going to Extremes

Change is disconcerting. The speed of change in the health care and insurance industries has caused many of the individuals responsible for making decisions to reach radical and often unwise conclusions about their needed direction and future. Particularly in the case of hospitals and physicians, alliances and consolidations are either the "thing to do" or the "thing to avoid." Groups of independent physicians, seeking to exert economic leverage in negotiations with insurers, recruit each other into new business entities, often without any idea of how to organize themselves and operate financially. Too often, they lack the capital, management, and information technology, not to mention the vision, that are the critical elements of business success. Yet they plunge ahead and join every kind of consortium, practice management company, physician-hospital organization (PHO), independent practice association (IPA), and whatever other alphabet soup entity offers them the promise of gaining back the decision-making control they feel they have lost. When groups of physicians try to form into integrated medical groups, they often overlook the need for the core ingredients that bind the organization together: stability of culture and of management. In resentment of nonphysician businesspeople whom they perceive as taking away the dollars that were once theirs in caring for people, physicians tend to believe that they are infallible. Their legacy is the ruin of far too many emergent health care organizations.

On the other side of the ledger are physicians who naively believe they can resist both the forces of managed care in particular and the forces of change in general, trusting to patient loyalty. From isolation and naiveté to radical ritual and organizational birthing and coupling, physicians seem to be struggling with the question and future of their identity in a world of transformation from caregiving to business considerations.

A similar pitfall awaits hospitals and other "integrated delivery systems" attempting to figure out how to conduct business efficiently and economically. Merging together a string of community hospitals that traditionally have either competed with, or have had no relationship with, each other makes little sense unless there is an underlying business rationale. Neither does it make sense to remain totally isolated, which some institutions do because they believe they are insulated from the forces of change by geography or patient loyalty, or because they believe they are too big or important to have their future jeopardized as academic medical centers.

Pitfall 2: The Need to Control Everything

Particularly in the world of not-for-profit and nonprofit organizations, there is a preoccupation with controlling all decision making. This is particularly true when it comes to relationships between physicians and hospitals. Hospital executives forget that it is doctors who put patients in hospitals or make referrals to their ancillary services. In the creation of the vast majority of physician-hospital partnerships, there is paranoia that physicians will do things that aren't in the interest of the institution or the health care system. The partnerships that work best are the ones in which physicians are the majority controllers of governance, regardless of who puts up the money for the partnership. Unless the trust problem is solved at a cultural and governance level, most of these partnerships either fail to attain their full potential or just plain fail.

Hospitals face similar dilemmas when confronting their own infrastructure. Most hospitals, particularly large academic medical centers, are labyrinths of conflicting fiefdoms and bureaucracies. They have a limited ability to retool their thinking to face radical restructuring of the way in which health care business is being done. Hospitals find themselves unable to eliminate their own internal barriers to change because they have rooted themselves in middle management infrastructures that inhibit creativity and empowerment. Combined with the reluctance to focus on the marketing of their services as a product brand rather than as a traditional inpatient facility, these entities are unprepared to face merged payers that exercise greater and greater competitive leverage over premium dollars. Far too often, administration seems to be unable to get out of its own way. That resistance is proving fatal to its longevity and health.

Pitfall 3: Putting Business before Caring

The preoccupation with turning health care into a commodity and a business has left many payers and institutions rudderless in terms of their mission and vision. They forget that they are in business because customers want quality care and personalized attention, and all of the focus on processes and outcomes and earnings takes them away from their roots and their success. Perhaps no better illustration exists than the advertising campaign by a major insurer touting itself as being in the "business of caring." "Caring" and "business" are the two preoccupations of the health care system, but the priority is still on delivering customer-focused care.

The formula for business success in health care and in just about every industry is based on providing a service or selling a product that the customer wants to buy. Commoditization of health care is too often synonymous with depersonalization, which is the very element that has caused the overwhelming backlash against the inevitable tide of managed care.

This problem is not limited to insurers; it also besets physicians who are being lured by the opportunity of selling their practices for immediate economic gratification. In the flurry over quick cash and stock, too many physicians are forgetting to concentrate on what made their practices successful in the first place—accessibility, quality, and personalized attention. The new breed of physicians coming out of medical school want and may well be entitled to more regular lifestyles, but medicine, beyond its obsession with technology and business opportunity, is still practiced one patient at a time.

Companies and practitioners that forget the basics of health care as a service business will find themselves without the very patients on which they count for their livelihoods.

Insurers, physicians, and institutions must learn how to cope with the needed economies that make the delivery and financing of health care more efficient, but they must also remember that service and quality are the ultimate differentiators of those who will succeed from those who will fail.

It is perhaps no accident, then, that the newly emerging group of local integrated physician and hospital companies delivering a managed care product rank near the top when it comes to customer perception about their quality. The national insurers and practice management companies need to strike a reasonable balance in the business versus caring equation. Health care may be integrating and consolidating faster than predicted by all but the most visionary executives, but the winners will ultimately be the entities that can create a culture that is care centered rather than business preoccupied.

Pitfall 4: Failure to Focus on the Essentials of Customer Service

Hospitals and physicians have often operated somewhat myopically when it comes to thinking about their patients as customers. Bricks and mortar and technology have always seemed to be more important than identifying the products and services that patients want to buy, at a price they want to pay, and with locations and hours that are convenient. An excellent illustration occurs in the field of obstetrics and gynecology, in which many of these physicians fiercely resist the development of holistic health care models catering to women's health in a much broader context than merely delivering babies and meeting the gynecological needs of patients.

They raise warning signals about deteriorating quality when the use of physician extenders are touted, and they cringe when massage, nutrition, and other preventive health concerns are put forward involving a partnership with nonphysician practitioners.

Service issues also abound when it comes to the health insurance and managed care industry. The products offered in the marketplace too often reflect the limits of the payment and information systems rather than being driven by the needs of employers and consumers. By managing cost rather than reengineering care, we are missing the point: Health care product is value driven; the best technology and the most brilliant physicians will not overcome mediocre or inattentive patient service or limited access. If a physician practice takes six weeks to schedule appointments or if the practice doesn't understand that patients need extended hours to cope with family and work schedules, the best product won't make up for these deficiencies.

Payers entering the Medicare and Medicaid managed care arenas are also learning about how service as a priority affects business success or failure. Medicaid managed care must form alliances with the community and with the human services infrastructure that supports this population. They must reach out to patients in new ways with culturally appropriate messages and materials. Medicare patients, a class that is only now beginning to grudgingly accept managed care, require significant education and personalized attention to help them use complicated managed care systems that may require referrals and authorization to obtain services.

Market research, customer feedback, staff training, and education are priorities that cannot be neglected, and they are opportunities to reach out to new customers while focusing on patient retention. Because physicians are able to exercise great influence over patient behavior, insurers will have to take seriously complaints about inaccurate data, late payment, and bureaucratic processes for care authorization from the very physicians on whom they are dependent for their competitive success.

Pitfall 5: Lack of Leadership and Vision

The last pitfall is probably the greatest and encompasses the first four. Many of the managed care companies operating as publicly traded companies have a vision that is narrowly focused on shareholder accountability. While this vision may mean an obsession with business needs before and above anything else, it *does* provide a framework for planning and for making decisions.

The rapid changes affecting the organization and delivery of care itself from the physician and hospital perspective has left many of these institutions in confusion. They pursue conflicting goals, undertake short-term strategies, get paranoid when they feel they are giving up too much control, and fail to appreciate that there is a need for decisiveness, boldness, and pride in what they deliver. Leadership and vision require new skill sets, with new talent that needs to be embraced and integrated rather than perceived as threatening. Physicians, who traditionally have been loyal to hospitals, need to be courted and empowered rather than controlled. As difficult as it may be to accomplish, tightly knit, clubby networks of trustees and old-line management may need to be replaced by those who understand that staying competitive means adopting a new set of values and a new business culture.

For payers, the challenge is to remember that health care decisions must be driven to the greatest extent possible by local market conditions and relationships. "One size does not fit all," either in terms of an insurance product or a reimbursement methodology for a contracting physician organization. Protecting turf is a sure recipe for mediocrity and failure; accepting challenges and being open to new ideas harbors the seeds for success.

Prescription for Action Strategies

- Be prepared to look at your organization—its infrastructure, empowerment levels, core competencies, and glaring deficiencies—with an unbiased lens. Think about bringing some outside "woodcutters" into the organization with strategic and business competencies in the areas where the organization is weakest (for example, managed care leadership for hospitals; provider and customer leadership for insurers).
- Assess your organization's ability and success in participating as part of a partnership or venture. If control or indecision are the major themes that run through these types of initiatives, fix the problem.
- Have the board of trustees, executive committee, or management council perform an internal assessment of the management leadership of the organization, with the help of outside evaluators if necessary. If you don't think your team can lead, then the rest of the competitive industry and the general business community won't see them as leaders either.
- Get an external viewpoint on what your customers (physicians, enrollees, or patients) think of your product in terms of brand identity, service, quality, accessibility, and price—and listen to the answers. Solicit opinions from current as well as departed customers and vendors to round out the analysis.
- Have each of your managers prepare a five- to ten-page written analysis of the organization's strengths, weaknesses, opportunities, and threats. Also have them identify one major risk-taking activity that they are willing to spearhead within the next year. If they are unable to identify one, they are not evolving and neither is your company. This process will help you find out if their vision equates with overall organizational vision, direction, and leadership. If nobody is really identifying challenges, then it's time to introduce an iconoclast into the company.

CONCLUSION

The concept of health care as a business, rather than a set of services to meet the care needs of consumers and communities, has resulted in a need to refocus on goals and objectives for caregivers and facilities. Physicians and hospitals must take a hard look at themselves and reevaluate their priorities in terms of market competitiveness and business survival.

This process has proven both painful and difficult for the many who are invested in their roles as fiduciaries or who believe that patient care is their only concern.

If health care is truly being reshaped to be packaged and sold as a commodity in the marketplace, then the dynamics that govern the marketing of products—branding of identity, differentiation of value, and meeting the needs of customers—become the primary objectives. For our health care system to remain dynamic, we must embrace the evolution and not run away from it, keeping in mind that the ultimate judge of the quality of health care services will be the degree to which the needs of a volatile and conflicting set of customers continue to be met.

2

Design Architecture Symptoms and Prescriptions for the Healing Enterprise

"Leaders of our hospital claim that it was designed by geniuses to be run by morons. But we know that just the opposite is true."

—Department manager of an academic medical center

Why is your health care organization designed to *constrain* effective implementation of your strategy for achieving market leadership?

When confronted with this question, most health care leaders will quickly respond—with some righteous indignation—that *our* health care organization is not designed to constrain strategy. And, of course, they are right! *Your* health care organization is not designed to constrain strategy. It just happens. The inflexibility, inconsistency, diminishing market share, endless internal turf battles, variable patient/customer service, employee frustration, and limited strategic progress are largely the unintended consequence of *lack of design.*

In our experience, health care organizations are *not* designed; their design is most often a random function of tradition, convenience, financial incentives, shrinking reimbursement, and the daily politics of attempting to respond to patients, providers, payers, managers, and employees without wobbling out of control. Most health care organizations reap the benefits and pay the costs of such just-in-time design. In forgiving noncompetitive environments, organizational survival can continue with such courting of chaos. The health care environment, however, is no longer forgiving of unpredictable business performance and clinical outcomes. In a profession built on the precept of "do no harm," random design is a prescription for organizational suicide in the new and changing world of health care in this country.

While the pace of change—and concurrent need for innovative implementation strategies—in the health care environment has markedly accelerated for at least the last 15 years, the design of most health care organizations has remained essentially the same or evolved only incrementally. And if the design of your health care organization is not in clear and consistent alignment with your strategic intent, misalignment inevitably amplifies imbalance and constrains momentum as your health care organization spins forward.

As in-house scientists of organizational behavior (that is, leaders), how can you assess possible gaps—misalignment—between the design of your health care organization and your strategic plan to achieve market leadership?

Our experience as professionals, managers, clinicians, and out-of-house scientists of organizational behavior (that is, consultants) tells us each day that a meaningful diagnosis of any misalignment between strategy and design must begin with dialogue. There can be no end to this dialogue. Without it, your health care organization will die as surely as random design leads to organizational decline.

Almost every health care leader believes in—or espouses a belief in—dialogue. But dialogue about what? We must have a continuing dialogue about how people and systems interact within an organization to achieve balance and momentum—how they interact to produce preferred outcomes and market leadership. Design at its best provides a rhetoric—a tool for influencing the future of your health care organization—that addresses those areas of organizational life of mutual concern both to the individual participants and to the organization as a whole. And while there can be no end to dialogue, the conversation must constantly focus on the critical few areas of mutual concern. Otherwise, chaos, entropy, competition, randomness, and narcissism—take your choice—will distract us from the hard work of reaching for market leadership.

THE ELEMENTS OF DESIGN ARCHITECTURE

Our experience across many health care organizations—big and small; integrated and stand-alone; local, regional, and national; domestic and foreign-based—has led us to identify six critical areas of *design architecture* (figure 2-1) that determine both clinical outcomes and business results:

1. Information
2. Structure
3. Rewards
4. Work Processes
5. People
6. Learning Systems

FIGURE 2-1. Six Critical Areas of Design Architecture

Information

Information can be divided into three components:

- The *type of information* provided or accessible to members of the organization in order to fulfill their roles and responsibilities
- The *critical measures* used to assess performance—results and process
- The *technology* and platforms required to connect people with the necessary information

Structure

Structure includes

- The way people are organized *horizontally,* such as service lines, locations, and patterns of collaboration between internal customers and suppliers
- The way people are organized *vertically,* including functions, departments, reporting relationships, and cost centers

Rewards

Rewards include the ways in which members of the organization are formally and informally compensated for their time and efforts:

- *Formal* rewards include monetary compensation, benefits, and promotions.
- *Informal* rewards include recognition activities, positive feedback, additional resources, greater access to information, involvement in decisions, "plum" projects, and a host of other nonmonetary "currencies."
- Any way in which the organization reinforces desired behaviors, performance, or attitudes is a reward.

Work Process

The work process includes

- A group of activities, decisions, or events that flow between or within functions, transforming a collection of inputs into outputs
- An exchange of information between customers and suppliers about their *requirements* that provides *feedback* on how to meet those requirements

People

The critical area of people encompasses

- The processes by which the organization acquires, develops, retains, and eventually parts ways with its members
- The human potential of the organization's members (for example, experience, competencies, and motivation)

Learning Systems

Learning systems are used to improve work by the following methods:

- Managing processes
- Using leading indicators to make timely decisions
- Continuously revisiting process design
- Gathering data from customers, suppliers, employees, and other stakeholders
- Partnering with customers and suppliers
- Seeking strategic alliances

Learning systems are also used to improve people's capabilities by

- Increasing access to information
- Providing training and resources

- Creating a climate of openness and trust
- Building ongoing performance feedback loops into the organization

SYMPTOMS OF MISALIGNMENT

Through our intensive investigation within client health care organizations, we have discovered repeating patterns of organizational behavior that are clear and reliable *symptoms of misalignment* between one or more of these areas and the health care organization's strategic intent. Our hope is that sharing these stories of poor or absent design will promote a dialogue within your health care organization regarding similar symptoms of misalignment. Such dialogue can lead to a cogent, mutually agreed-upon diagnosis of symptoms—gaps in alignment—and enable custom design of action strategies within your health care organization.

Symptom 1: Confusing the "What" and "How" of Planning

Developing strategic intent requires planning what the organization will be in future years. Will we become a rehabilitation facility? Will we shift from acute to ambulatory care? Will we form a strategic alliance to achieve economies of scale or remain autonomous in our competition for market share? Will we own physician practices, develop management service organizations, or negotiate through a PPO, IPA, or PHO to achieve the best contracts? Developing strategic intent in the face of escalating uncertainty requires courage to clearly answer these questions with inadequate data and imperfect analysis. A vigorous strategic intent drives a

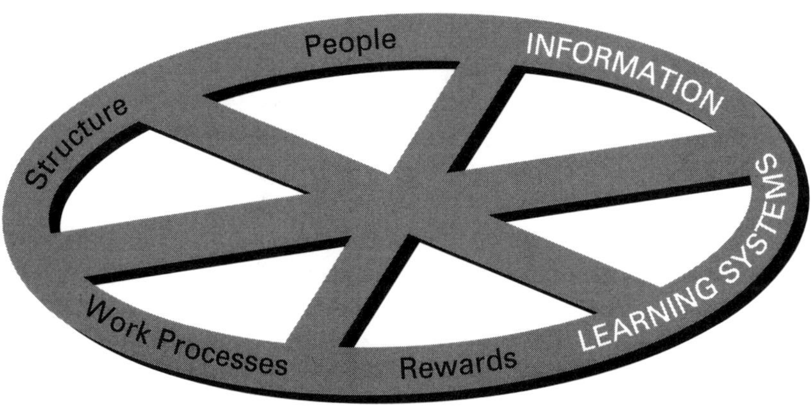

stake in the map of future possibilities and states we are "this" and not "that." Strategic intent targets *what* a health care organization's positioning for market leadership will be, what diverse customer requirements will be, and what core competencies will be developed to transform today's possibility into tomorrow's market reality.

By contrast, operational planning should determine *how* we will realize our strategic intent. It responds to challenges such as: How will we meet and exceed anticipated customer requirements? *How* will we convert, build, or sell off current facilities to align with *what* we are to become? Rigorous operational planning defines a path to reach the stake in the map of strategic intent.

There are a number of ways in which health care organizations confuse the what and how of strategy and operational planning. Many organizations' idea of strategic planning is simply to review last year's performance and set unrealistic goals of a 10 to 20 percent reduction in this or improvement in that without any changes in the existing infrastructure and critical systems of the organization. Other organizations proclaim a desire for "breakthrough" performance in new areas while devoting inadequate resources to core competency redevelopment, thus assuring incremental improvement at best. When there is a misalignment or confusion of strategic planning with operational planning, direction is uncertain and momentum is lost.

Diagnostic Questions to Ask in Your Health Care Organization

- What is different about your position in the local/regional health care market compared to three years ago?

Prescription for Action Strategies

- Convene a series of "how" workshops to focus management attention and behavior on defining just "how" each function will contribute to a strategic goal.
- Syndicate strategic thinking throughout the organization. Without such thinking, contributions to strategy will be random and the tendency to narrowly focus on functional and departmental success will be maintained, whatever the areas of misalignment may be.
- Be honest (with yourself and with others) about what business you are in. One way of defining this critical issue is to ask what are you *really* getting paid for? For example, perhaps payers are paying for complete medical records since the measure of service itself is beyond our technologies. If this is so, what business would you be in?

- Does this difference reflect defined strategic intent ("what") or simply incremental response to environmental demands for service delivery ("how")?
- Do you know what the strategic intent of your health care organization is for the next three years?
- Do you know how long-range operational planning will support specific action strategies reflecting changes that your strategic intent demands?

If you have difficulty in answering these questions without extensive excavation of documents, meeting notes, and the private thinking of senior management, consider confusion of "what" and "how" as a confirmed symptom of misalignment in your health care organization.

Symptom 2: Information Addiction

Some health care organizations fall in love with all planning processes and make planning for change a year-round event. In such organizations, there is a sense that you can never gather too much market data, customer feedback, or employee input. In this information age, information often becomes an obsession unto itself. We mail out surveys daily and agonize over the response rates. Some customers receive two to three surveys a week on a whole range of topics from many different functions, floors, or services in a health care organization.

Organizations that keep gathering data usually fear the inherent risk of making a decision. They put off the tough decision with the excuse that they need more data, more data, more data. Organizations like this become mesmerized with information. The result is that the strategic planning, operational planning, and all planning processes never conclude and implementation strategies never move beyond perpetual pondering.

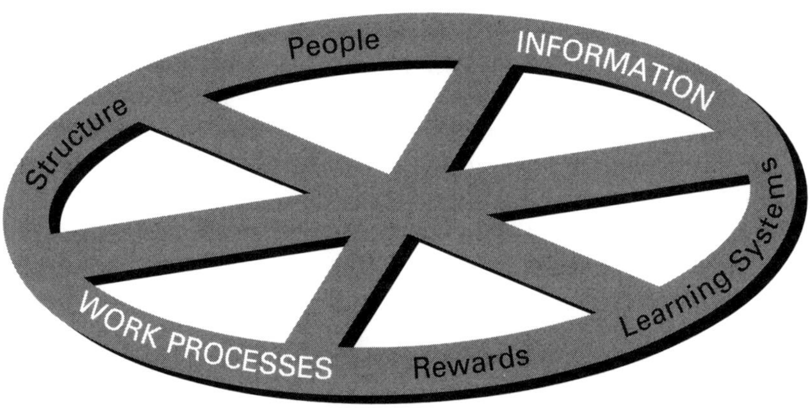

Health care organizations are especially vulnerable to this symptom as a consequence of the medical mandate to "do no harm." They are used to performing scientific searches for information that will predict clinical outcomes with a certainty—a certainty that businesses, especially businesses in turbulent times, can rarely realize.

Robust planning processes must have an advanced analytical process to digest all the information that comes in. Only then can meaningful conclusions be reached and acted upon. These conclusions need to be communicated to senior management and syndicated across the organization on a regular basis with an analysis of trends and summaries of key findings.

This is because whatever the value of data gathered and transformed into information, assumptions must be drawn, goals must be set, and decisions must be made in any effective planning process. If there is no action or outcome as a consequence of planning, where is the value? There must be a punctuation—a moment of conclusion—or the addiction to information, like any addiction, will only deteriorate into a perpetual cry for more, more, more.

We must treat information as a critical organizational asset. We must demand that we receive a return on our investment as measured by improved performance. While not every health care organization can or should have a chief information officer, it is essential in these days of connectivity, integration, clinical report cards, tightening margins, and demands for faster and faster cycle times and for ever more responsive core processes that *someone* be accountable for a substantial return on investments in information technology, systems, software, and service. If current information systems are providing endless but useless information—making action difficult or impossible—then it is time to redesign the information process. Otherwise, you will suffer the long-term erosion and loss of function that accompanies any untreated addiction.

Diagnostic Questions to Ask in Your Health Care Organization

- Do you receive information that is too late or too ambiguous to guide you in your day-to-day improvement efforts?
- Are you continuously asked for information but rarely receive feedback on the meaning or value of information gathered?
- Does your information technology exceed the capacity of all but the most sophisticated users?
- Does your information services function/department treat you like an idiot for expecting timely, responsive, and friendly service?
- Are people afraid to make a critical decision in your health care organization without continuous demand for more information?
- Is endless data debate considered a value-added activity in your health care organization?

Prescription for Action Strategies

- Require that all reports of more than two pages have a half-page executive summary of key points for the readers' review. (One *Fortune* 500 company established this policy after a pilot project in which a widely distributed weekly report of 10 pages included several repetitions of Lewis Carroll's poem "Jabberwocky" for all of page 7. No one noted this insertion, presumably because no one read as far as page 7!)
- Establish clear and aggressive decision deadlines independent of the longing for infinite analysis of unavailable data.
- Acknowledge (often) that the quality and rigor of information/analysis available will often be insufficient to guarantee success, but that in an environment of accelerating change, inaction *can* assure failure. That is, increased information does not always decrease risk if delay costs money.

If you cannot just say "no" to these questions, your health care organization is probably experiencing the loss of momentum and escalating imbalance accompanying most addictions.

Symptom 3: Measurement Malaise

In the 1960s, some of us believed "we are what we eat." For health care organizations in the 1990s, "we are what we measure." Our measures tell us what we value and what we choose to ignore, either by intent or neglect. For example, until very recently there has been little concerted effort in most hospitals to measure mistakes in the process of

distributing medication. Given the risk of litigation and the absence of serious tort reform, the choice to ignore such known occurrences can be understood, but this choice remains unacceptable to those truly concerned with both patient care and business performance.

But there is no management without measurement. With measures that are not aligned to strategy, process, operations, and outcomes, there is only mismanagement. Many health care organizations routinely introduce new strategies, new products and services, redesigned processes, and new goals to achieve breakthrough performance but continue to use the same old measures to track progress. Seldom do they evaluate whether the old measures are relevant to the new health care organization in the changing health care environment.

For example, in some health care organizations, maintenance measures the number of orders completed but does not prioritize requests for service. In others, the number of stat labs delivered within a given cycle time is measured, but there are no measures for determining the difference between what has become routine "stat" and truly urgent needs for information. In still others, access to appointments through a call center is measured, but satisfaction with advice provided by telephone is not. In many health care organizations, "within budget" is a key measure, while measures of internal customer satisfaction with how that budget has been deployed are sadly missing. In some heavily unionized organizations, management measures complaints while union membership measures any change in assigned duties, but measures of contribution and productivity become the roadkill of divisive politics. In a number of academic medical centers, measures of length of stay are calculated with great care while the cost of care provided by each physician is either not calculated or hidden like a state secret.

Measures must be transparently linked to the strategic intent, or people at all levels will assume that existing measures are about command, control, and the convenience of those measuring. Measures must encapsulate the strategic intent and provide for clarity and reduced confusion at lower organizational levels. This will facilitate alignment of all aspects of operations—clinical, business, and service—to support and achieve the strategic intent.

Measurement is sometimes feared because it promotes accountability. Accountability equates to responsibility for actions taken. Responsibility can, of course, have both positive and negative consequences associated with it. In reviewing progress against established measures of both processes and outcomes, there must be a built-in mechanism to reduce the fear associated with measurements. The review process must build up both individual and system ability to react quickly to measurement results and put action plans into place to correct any obvious deviations or undesirable trends. If measurement is mostly used as a whip and a weapon rather than as a constructive tool for change, mutual concern for outcomes will be sacrificed at the altar of individual interest.

Most health care organizations sorely neglect measurement, at least in part because they have no agreed-upon measurement architecture to guide them in the development and application of measures. Rick Waks, president of RAW Consulting and Development, has helped all of us to understand that since the goal of design and redesign is aligned change, you must develop aligned measures. Measuring the performance of a task by an individual is, of course, different than measuring the performance of a process by a group of people or the performance of a strategy by a whole hospital. The first is a *leading indicator* of the subsequent *lagging indicators*. Measures must fit together in a way that allows for comparison, predictability, and insight up, down, and across your health care organization. This is called a *measurement architecture*, as illustrated in figure 2-2.

But good measurement is still hard to do. Too frequently we measure things because they are easy to measure rather than because they are important to measure. It is often easier to measure efficiency than effectiveness, just as it is often easier to measure volume than contribution. But what is most important to your health care organization is to develop the discipline as leaders, managers, and staff to measure what matters because measurement makes things concrete, visible, and difficult to ignore. We must keep reminding ourselves that what gets measured gets managed effectively and efficiently.

Diagnostic Questions to Ask in Your Health Care Organization

- Are cost, cost, and cost the only measures that really count in your health care organization?
- Do you, your department, your function, your service, and your organization measure your contribution to the health care organization's strategic intent? If not, how do you know if you're doing the right things?
- How are measures of internal customer satisfaction with products and services developed and used to leverage new behaviors and in the design of improved processes?
- Given that speed is a key component of competitive advantage in most industries, does your health care organization actively measure the cycle time of service/products from request to delivery?
- Does your health care organization have a means of measuring mistakes in clinical service delivery (for example, pharmacy, labs, or scheduling) as a foundation for true clinical quality improvement? If so, how do you protect your mistake makers and mistake finders?

FIGURE 2-2. **Leading Indicators and Lagging Indicators**

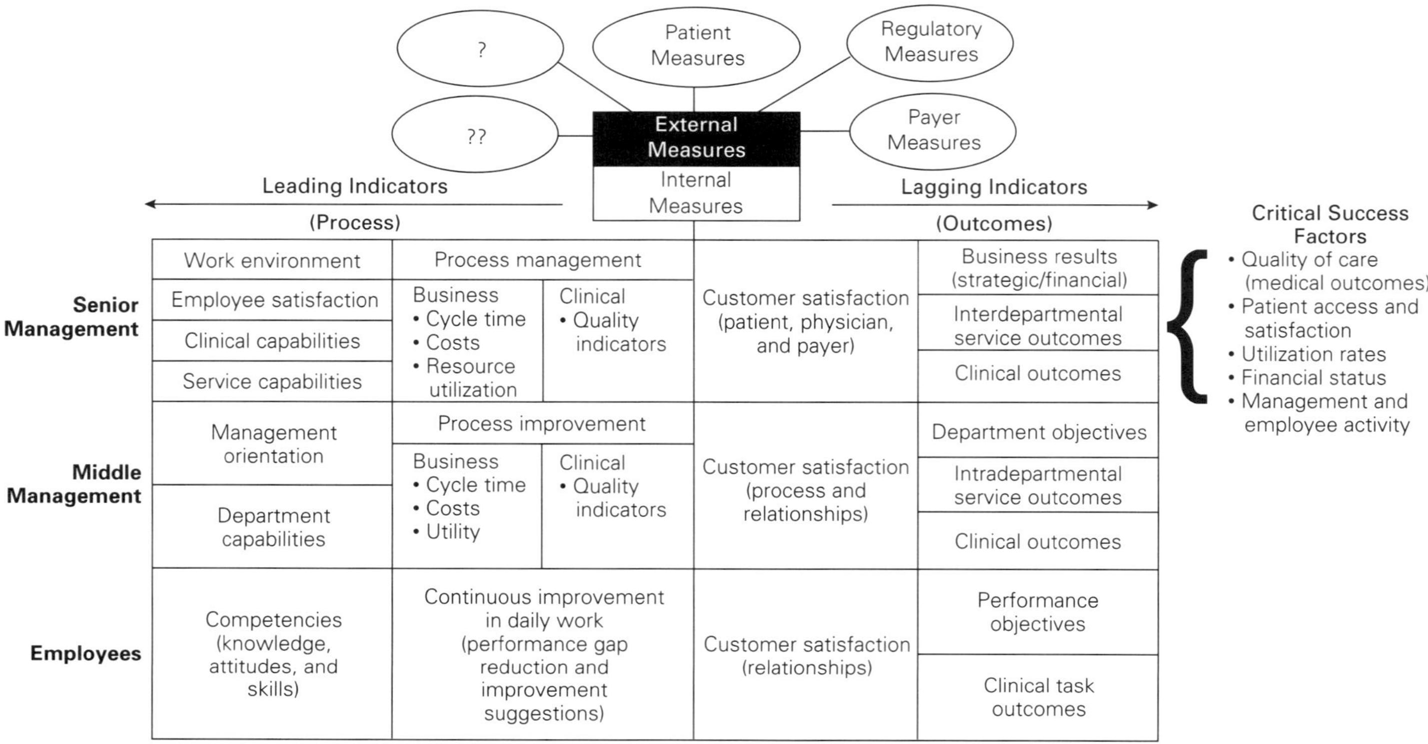

Prescription for Action Strategies

- Tie significant compensation of the leadership group to three to five key hospitalwide measures.
- Differentiate the critical few measures that should drive decisions in each function and department from the meaningless many that simply must be kept because the joint commission or some other regulatory body says you must.

- Is measurement a daily and weekly concern for your health care organization? (Or is it just an annual exercise to be survived and forgotten until the same time next year?)

If measurement is less than meaningful, there may be terrific momentum in your health care organization spinning toward an uncertain future, but there is also a strong probability that you will reach a destination only poorly aligned with your strategic intent.

Symptom 4: Tradition, Tradition, Tradition!

"That's not the way we do it around here . . ." is the death knell of many health care organizations that presume a glorious past will somehow assure a robust future. Innovation cannot thrive in a culture that has already discovered the truth in almost everything it does. *Veritas* is a great motto for a world-class university, but when *veritas* becomes *vanitas*, any real shift in strategic intent to meet the challenges of a changing health care environment is doomed by the rigidity, arrogance, and myopia of the often heard refrain: "That's not the way we do it around here."

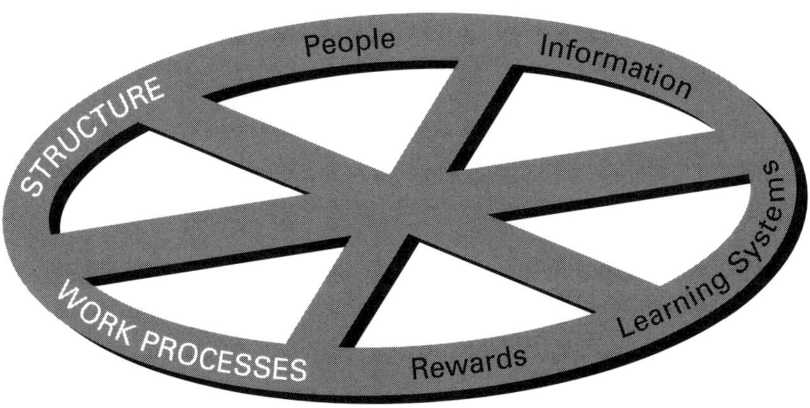

If you doubt the danger of this symptom of imbalance, it may be worth recalling the fall from industry leadership of two giants and the demise of a small quality-driven superstar.

General Motors, the world's largest business organization of the 1960s, continued to produce big cars despite the evidence of a size revolution in its own parking lots, filled with small, foreign-manufactured cars made by (then) unknown upstarts Honda and Toyota. The more courageous frontline workers told management that the day of the dinosaur had passed. By the 1980s GM was half the size of once upon a time. Why were the demigods of Detroit so blind, deaf, and dumb? "That's not the way we do it around here."

Ma Bell—AT&T—was the *only* game in town until 1984. Monopoly in telecommunications was fertile soil for tradition. Customer focus and corporate flexibility do not come easily when there is no consumer choice. Even with divestiture looming, AT&T was assured by the best consulting advice money could buy that the worst case scenario would be a 9 to 11 percent projected loss of world market share. After a decade of deregulation Ma Bell had lost 39 percent of world market to upstart start-ups like MCI, Sprint, and Microsoft. Whom to blame? Some suggested that executive leadership—first Charlie Brown and then Jimmy Olsen—had acted more like comic book characters then corporate warriors. But when author Dan Anderson personally consulted on implementing quality leadership (total quality management) at AT&T's corporate headquarters in Basking Ridge, New Jersey, in the late 1980s, the constant refrain was still: "That's not the way we do it around here."

And then there is the story of the Wallace Company, a small once-prosperous manufacturing company in Louisiana. Like most health care organizations today—no doubt including *your* health care organization—the Wallace Company claimed an uncompromising commitment to quality. Nothing was more important than the quality of products and services provided to its customers. Storyboards plastered the walls. Stories of staff dedication beyond the call of duty were told and retold to visitors from every industry. Quality had become a way of life—a tradition—at the Wallace Company. Anything that did not reflect a commitment to quality was not the Wallace way. In 1987 the Wallace Company won the prestigious Malcolm Baldrige National Quality Award, an award that many health care organizations will aspire to if they become eligible to compete. Even in the name of *quality*, however, "That's not the way we do it around here" may be more an epitaph than a preface to market leadership. The Wallace Company ended up in a Chapter 11 bankruptcy court in 1990.

Many say, "But health care is different," claiming our tradition of quality care is based on a commitment to patients and the best possible outcomes, not on making cars, telephones, widgets, and profit. Perhaps a few frequently encountered traditions (or are they nasty habits in

Prescription for Action Strategies

- Identify assumptions driving essential activities at each level of your health care organization.
- *Reverse* these assumptions and identify subsequent changes in behavior. Those that don't make a difference reflect expendable traditions.
- Construct a *sacred cow matrix* listing the "untouchable" assumptions/people/behaviors on one axis with the estimated cost for feeding these sacred cows on the other axis. Can you afford the upkeep?

disguise?) within health care organizations may speak to the dangers of imbalance, lost momentum, misalignment, and, ultimately, our cherished ideal of patient care.

Diagnostic Questions to Ask in Your Health Care Organization

- How often do ideas originating on the "front line" that challenge prevailing norms in your health care organization get discussed in senior management meetings?
- How difficult is it to shift work and tasks that do not require professional training from licensed to unlicensed personnel?
- Is "That's not how we do it around here" a common response to questions offered by new hires?

Symptom 5: The Knee Bone's Not *Connected to the . . .*

And the structure is *not* connected to either the strategy or the process of work. Frederick Taylor is often credited with being the father of the

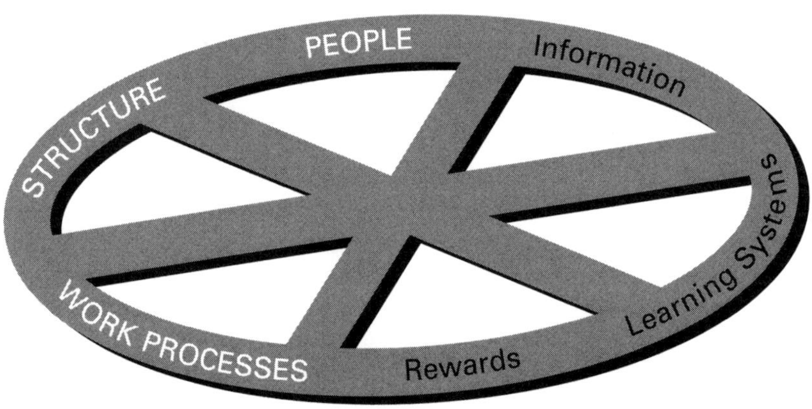

functional organization, first designed in the early years of this century. And while his purpose was to bring efficiency to emerging complex organizations, many health care organizations have embraced functional organization while rarely achieving the efficiency Taylor proposed. Despite years of implementing continuous quality improvement (CQI) in response to escalating patient expectations, payer requirements, and a mid-1980s mandate from the Joint Commission on the Accreditation of Healthcare Organizations, waste, redundancy, and functional management are healthy and well in most health care organizations (probably including your health care organization).

While most health care organizations and emerging health care systems are concerned with achieving *vertical* (functional) integration, it is the vertical organization that is often at the root of imbalance and lost momentum in serving key customer groups.

As health care business consultants, we have had frequent opportunity to listen to weekly senior management meetings of academic medical centers, community hospitals, urban specialty hospitals, and large physician group practices. Too often, it's like hearing reports from kingdoms of an empire with nothing in common beyond the shared desire to please the emperor with the isolated performance of their specific domain.

In one urban specialty hospital, for example, all of the vice presidents except the VP for finance complained about both the financial and clinical capacity and service of the healthcare information services (HIS) department for a number of years. Since the VP for finance routinely defended the quality, efficiency, and responsiveness of HIS, nothing changed until the organizational equivalent of an internal coup.

In a renowned academic medical center, the VP for patient care steadfastly refused to have nurses transport patients, pharmaceuticals, or medical records because "that's not what nurses are trained to do."

Simultaneously, the same VP refused to allow anyone but nurses to change beds, bathe patients, or make notes in medical records to preserve nursing jobs that could be performed as well but much less expensively by other staff members. Perhaps because this VP had more than 40 percent of all employees report to her function, nothing changed.

In many community hospitals, supervisors have given up requesting any but the most routine services from other departments because it is simply easier to "do it yourself" or "do without" than suffer the delay of waiting for a department head or VP to approve any change in procedure or practice.

In each of these cases, there is no process for translating strategic or operational goals into *horizontal* cross-functional collaboration that transcends turf warfare, professional prerogative, and functional myopia. Too often, ownership of service to the patients, providers, and other constituents is constrained by the very functional structures that were supposed to facilitate efficiency and productivity.

Prescription for Action Strategies

- Identify or select senior-level owners of core processes with direct linkage to critical organization strategies.
- Create core process maps beginning with the external customer identifying activities in reverse order.
- Map the processes associated with traditional health care functions (such as admitting, scheduling, staffing, and procurement) and define the *value contribution* to each core process.
- Establish core process measures and hold owners accountable for progress against these measures.

Diagnostic Questions for Your Health Care Organization

- Do you know what the three most critical core processes of your health care organization are? Do you know what business you are in?
- How does your department/function support each of these core processes?
- Are vice presidents and department directors given performance evaluations by internal customers of their functions and departments?
- Does your health care organization have service-level agreements to assure standards of cross-functional quality, cycle time, and service?
- Has the structure of your health care organization changed to meet the challenges in your local and our national health care environment?

Symptom 6: Arrogance of Assuming Universal Competence

While health care is arguably the largest and most critical business in the United States, it remains the only major industry that (until very recently) seems to believe that it can—organizationally speaking—be extraordinarily competent in every function and service. In the past decade, *Fortune* 500 companies have begun to define themselves more and more in terms of *core competencies*—be it innovative marketing, operations excellence, research and development, accounting sophistication, customer focus, or technology. In this context, a core competency reflects world-class capacity in a given domain. It is important to note that *none* of the *Fortune* 500 companies are widely recognized for more than *two* core competencies. Many organization scientists argue that having more than two core competencies is probably impossible in today's competitive environment.

So what does this have to do with the arrogance of many health care organizations? Other industries have achieved a more mature realization that if they cannot be the very best at everything they do, perhaps they should buy or lease competencies and capacities from other firms that specialize in just those areas where true excellence is difficult or costly to achieve independently. That is, if you have a great fastball and a fine slider, maybe borrowing a curveball and a knuckler are just the ticket in the market leadership game. Many health care organizations, however, are prone to a number of actions that reflect more hubris than intelligence in estimating the real business-world value of core competence.

The first such action is in health care's resistance to creative outsourcing of functions to other firms with the needed competence. While food services and billing are more and more frequently contract functions, where is the outsourcing of other "hotel" functions: information technology, facilities management, diverse purchased services, marketing, and public relations? What is the cost of acting as though no one else can deliver the support systems that might enable more efficient and effective delivery of patient care?

The second way in which many health care organizations express their arrogance is in their insistence on remaining "multispecialty/full-service" general hospitals despite the reality that there are only one or two service niches in which they do (or could) truly excel. In one hospital, for example, 80 percent of its margin and reputation were attributed to its orthopedic services, but more than 40 percent of its resources were dedicated to "full-service" delivery. In another, cardiac services plays the same role. In a third, OB/Gyn is the fastball that supports mediocre pitching in other areas. And despite the rush toward mergers, acquisitions, and fully integrated health care systems—especially in the West and Northeast, the sought-after economies of scale have rarely

Prescription for Action Strategies

- Define one or two core competencies of your health care organization.
- Define one or two *different* core competencies of other health care organizations in your area. Open up a cross-organization dialogue on sharing competencies and reducing waste.
- Develop and send out requests for proposals to vendors for all clinical support, finance, human resource, and operating functions to determine the true need to maintain in-house delivery capacity.
- Ask department directors to design their function in a soon-to-be-built new facility across town. Reward innovation, not duplication.

been realized; duplication of services thrives under one supposed corporate roof.

The root cause of this organizational arrogance seems to be a failure to recognize just what business we are in. If we cannot identify our core business processes, how can we develop and sustain the core competencies needed to sustain our future position in the market? Unless we confront the reality that we are in the business of patient care (or managing physician practices, or managed care contracting), then the effort to be in many businesses inevitably means an erosion of the core competency potential of your health care organization. And in health care, how long can we afford to live in the business land of "what might have been" when our access to capital and reimbursement will never again be "what was once upon a time"?

Diagnostic Questions to Ask in Your Health Care Organization

- How often has your health care organization made site visits in other industries to benchmark world-class processes?
- If your health care organization claims to be the best in your city, state, region, or in the country, do you have externally validated data to back up such a claim?
- What does your health care organization do poorly compared to other health care organizations in your market?

Symptom 7: Mad Hatter's Performance at Wonderland Hospital

In contrast to information addiction (symptom 2), some health care organizations respond to the accelerating demands in the health care

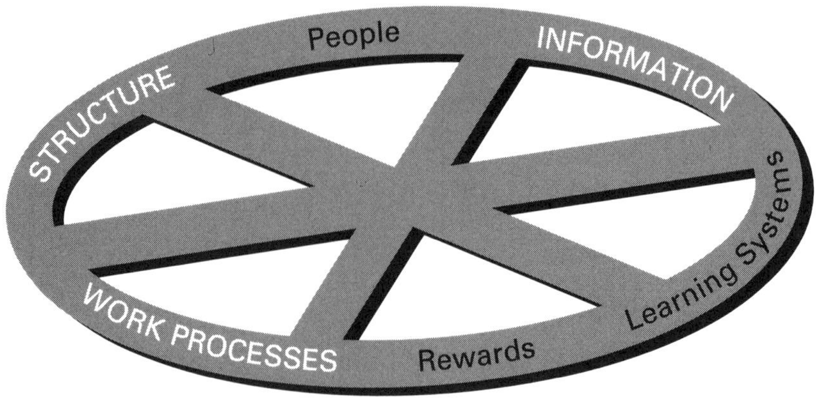

environment with both real and symbolic action, communicating that "we're late, we're late, we're late for a very important date." The impulsive health care organization rushes to solutions prematurely without the due diligence that complex problem solving demands even in the most accelerated environments.

For example, women's health centers would seem to be a right idea at the right time for the right population of consumers. Being right—and even righteous—in defense of the health of women is beyond reproach. In too many hospitals, however, the failure to ask the market—women to be served—whether such a separate service was economically feasible has not been assessed as a *business* rather than a *political* decision. In today's lean—and sometimes mean—health care environment, we must either be willing to sustain such social commitments despite the cost of poor performance or take the time for business analysis of whether the local market will justify the investment of diminishing revenues. Otherwise—as has happened too often—the integrity of your health care organization's community commitment and the wisdom of your business decisions will be suspect at best.

The health care environment is littered with the regrets, second thoughts, and brilliant hindsight of acquiring physician group practices. If women's health centers at least seemed right in so many ways, to our mind the purchase of many practices seemed wrong and a risky business at the very best for many health care organizations. What were they thinking about—beyond the obvious wish to corner as much of the patient/managed care contract market as possible? Had they never met the physicians they hoped to own? The too frequent failure to assess the currencies of motivation—beyond cash—that drive many physicians has left hospitals everywhere with unmanageable assets, unrecoverable debt, and resentful employees. While we (the authors) have resisted the temptation to psychopathologize organizational behavior, it does indeed seem that many such acquisitions are the product of hostility toward physicians who refuse to be controlled by hospital administrations despite whatever euphemisms of partnership may drive such arrangements. It has been said that managing physicians is like herding cats. Indeed.

While this may seem a severe indictment of hospitals' acting on the understandable impulse to gain some leverage in competitive markets, we have begun to see a parallel impulse in a number of physician—staff model group practices. Many are eagerly negotiating to have full management responsibility for both clinical and nonclinical support staff, including union members. Clearly, hospitals have not cornered the market on the impulse to act beyond competence. Indeed.

And then there is merger mania, which is not really an *impulse* disorder, since getting bigger and integrated vertically, horizontally, and every way possible *is* often a necessary strategy to establish competitive and negotiating position. What does seems impulsive, however, is the number of mergers that neglect the planning needed to realize the intended "economies of scale" and that also neglect to address the predictable (and costly) culture clash of blending fiercely independent health care organizations under a single corporate mantle.

In one full-asset merger of nationally known academic medical centers, the total number of vice presidents actually *increased* following the merger and remained constant following budget reductions of more than 12 percent of total operating expenses. While the visible symbolism of maintaining administrative overhead enraged those delivering and receiving pink slips, the transparent reality of maintaining distinct support services (that is, maintenance, clinical engineering, labs, and emergency rooms) makes next year's reduction in *clinical* staffing as inevitable as it is unnecessary. And while some insiders loudly proclaim that economies of scale may be possible in the long term, local labor organizers are seizing the short-term opportunity to launch a preemptive campaign.

If the cost of merging two organizations on paper—without functional and service integration—is at least ostensibly measurable, what is the immeasurable human cost of failing to blend the best of merging hospitals into a vital, robust culture that resonates with pride in service to patients, providers, and each other? Too many mergers seem like a marriage of passionate but naive adolescents for whom real differences in background, status, race, religion, and family tradition (see symptom 4 above) are considered only after entrenched patterns of conflict are established.

In one such marriage, the groom hospital had a long and respected teaching tradition. Resident physicians used almost every possible lab test to rule out even the most obscure diagnosis in order to avoid that awful moment at morning rounds when the attending physician sarcastically would inquire, "Tell me, doctor, did you consider testing for . . ."

Prescription for Action Strategies

- Rely on external, focused expertise to provide due diligence on ventures that seem to present immediate opportunities.
- Assess the true cost of not moving forward as rapidly as possible.
- Diagnose the root cause of the urgency to act now.

At the bride hospital, a new cost-conscious teaching tradition had begun to take hold. Attending physicians would patiently inquire of the resident physician, "What symptoms led you to order such a costly test?"

Within this same marriage, leadership at the bride hospital had established a tradition that all meetings would start and stop on time (an uncommon habit in the authors' health care experience). No one would dream of coming late to a meeting with a just-purchased hot cup of coffee—the warm comfort simply would not compensate for the cool reception. At the groom hospital, however, stragglers coming in 10 or 15 minutes late was the norm for meetings that almost always spilled over scheduled length anyway.

Now, two years into the marriage, residents are religious in ordering the most expensive tests at both hospitals, and meetings don't start on time at either!

Diagnostic Questions to Ask in Your Health Care Organization

- Are you in a merger that everyone but the lawyers already regrets?
- Have new ventures been initiated with current resources without significant consideration for the impact on current staffing and programs?
- Does the culture of your health care organization allow you to abandon an idea you are convinced is understudied and premature at best?
- If you have acquired physician practices, were the challenges of managing physicians adequately estimated?

Symptom 8: It's Who You Know That Matters Around Here

No design can (or even should) eliminate the give-and-take politics of human relationships in organizational life. The universal favor bank—*quid pro quo*—can be a very constructive force in assuring collaboration in the face of growing competitive pressures.

However, in many—perhaps most—of the hospitals we have worked with over the years, efficient response to legitimate, internal requests for services and products (not involving clinical emergencies) is *too* dependent on the personal as opposed to the process knowledge of how to get something done. In one hospital, knowing Steve in maintenance (and remembering his brand of Scotch at Christmas) is a condition of getting something fixed in a timely manner. In another, knowing Helen, the nurse manager on 2 East, is a condition for finding an available room for Dr. Jones in a time of high occupancy. And in still another hospital, playing golf with the executive vice president for operations is a condition for reconsideration of a budget request denied at a lower level in the chain of command.

Many may suggest that this is simply how organizations work and it behooves all of us to get to know the Steves and Helens of this world and to learn how to play golf at the earliest possible date. Maybe so. But in each case, the power of "who you know" is amplified by the absence of reliable, predictable, and knowable efficient work processes that would make the exercise of personal knowledge less vital to the delivery of service to our patients and each other.

Diagnostic Questions to Ask in Your Health Care Organization

- What would be the cost in delay, redundancy, and frustration if any 10 people in your health care organization contracted a week-long bout of the flu at the same time?
- How long does it take a reasonably intelligent, experienced new hire to get up to speed in your health care organization?
- Would you want to be held accountable for competent performance as a new hire in your health care organization?

Prescription for Action Strategies

- Have all managers create *process maps* based on what their direct reports indicate are the *actual* steps of the three most critical work processes from initiation to delivery of products, services, and information. These process maps should include "Call Helen (or Steve)"; "No one responds to inquiries during 'change of shift' from 3 to 4 P.M.; and "All requests after 10 A.M. on Friday will not receive a response before Monday at noon." In other words, managers need to flowchart reality, *not* policy or fantasy.
- If the "who you know" approach to work serves *most* of your health care organization well, consider ways to incorporate the current "going around the system" into the standard operating processes so that all can take advantage of the wisdom of the few ancients who already know everybody. Remember, there are often good reasons why people have learned to ignore or manipulate current work processes.
- Build in measurement and accountability so those who actually use the work processes as designed are rewarded—and not inadvertently punished—for compliance.

Symptom 9: We Are Family

This may be the big—and most injurious—lie of community hospitals everywhere. If we are family, how come Uncle George's role in the family just got outsourced? How come Cousin Betty just got laid off despite having two kids in college? How come Brother Barney and Sister Mary-Lou just left us in the lurch to accept a better offer from another family? Families are about affiliation; work is about achievement. Confusing two of the most important sources of identity in our lives contributes immeasurably to the rage, disappointment, resistance to change, and sometimes sabotage that characterizes so many hospitals that have promoted the myth of family at work.

In one small community hospital, the "family" metaphor had been central to maintaining a positive, motivated, and loyal work population for 20 years. As has been the case in many hospitals in our experience, the long-reigning CEO encouraged this framing of work relationships and, in turn, was almost universally regarded as the "good father" of both the hospital and of health care in the surrounding communities. Despite this approach, the hospital had been widely unionized for many years, consistent with many of the industries in a predominantly working-class community. As contracts were periodically renegotiated in the "golden trough" days of almost infinite reimbursement, hospital administration demonstrated its commitment to "family" by offering the most generous wages and benefits in the state.

However, when times changed and revenue dropped, the need for lower pay scales became apparent. As one wit noted: "How can we ever derive market value from an $18-an-hour cook?" The shift to tough negotiating was widely seen as a betrayal of the "family"; union leadership was unwilling to soften any position in the name of family, relying on the language of contracts and the threat of walkouts rarely heard at most dining-room tables. The hospital was *never* really a family, but the cost to culture and the bottom line of this well-meaning fable continues to be felt to this day.

In another large urban medical center, the commitment to the "family" of employees often came into conflict with the commitment to "patient care" and to "physician satisfaction." In hundreds of ways—both large and small—the convenience of employee family members seemed to transcend the needs for consistent, predictable service. Flexible scheduling of staff became an entitlement, not an occasional benefit of a good employer. The harried or occasionally abrasive physician's orders received lower priority. Poor productivity—sleeping in a closet; time-clock manipulation; excessive "sick" time—were acceptable norms, much as is the case in many families that affectionately tolerate the idiosyncratic behavior of a wayward child. A performance management system that recognized more than 80 percent of workers as performing "above average" combined with automatic cost-of-living adjustments constrained accountability and eliminated all threat of termination for any member of the family. What is the impact of such "family" behaviors on patient care? As the then chief operating officer commented in a personal aside to one of the authors: "I understand that our mission as a great hospital is to care for the infirm, the diseased, and the disabled, but I never dreamed that so many of those requiring such care would be our own employees while at work."

Prescription for Action Strategies

- If your health care organization still has an active family metaphor at work, kill it. Or when a real crisis in work comes, your health care organization may have more in common with the Mansons than the Waltons.
- Find a new—honest—way to frame the relationships of work that facilitates and rewards contribution and honest confrontation of poor performance. There are many possibilities. It does not matter so much what word is used, but what definition is given to the realities of working relationships in any industry, including health care. As has been widely noted in recent years, the *social contract* of work has dramatically shifted from that of the last generation. Health care leaders need to reflect this shift in their language and actions.
- Redesign your performance management system. Your patients, your providers, your payers, and your many able workers deserve the benefits and accountability of such redesign.

Diagnostic Questions to Ask in Your Health Care Organization

- Do people privately (or publicly) make fun of any reference to being a family?
- Does your performance management system rate more than 70 percent of workers as "above average"?
- Does your health care organization give preference to actual family members of current workers, whatever the human resources policy may say to the contrary?
- Is professional criticism taken as personal?

Symptom 10: What We Don't Know Won't Kill Us

It's ironic that organizations dedicated to delivering the fruits of medical science have been so consistently comfortable with management ignorance. Imagine your surgeon telling you, "What I don't know won't kill you." Yet despite the growing evidence that organizational learning may be the key to competitive advantage and market leadership in other industries, the overall rate of innovation, creative mistakes, nonprofessional staff development, and constructive confrontation in health care sadly lags behind many industries concerned with the delivery of services and products that your life does *not* depend upon.

While there is no formal research elucidating just why health care organizations often thwart rather than encourage innovation—and the many failed experiments that innovation usually demands—our experi-

ence leads us again and again to focus on the medical mandate to *do no harm*. In many health care organizations, this critical clinical injunction to do no harm is translated into the daily practice of *take no risk*. And without the encouragement of risk, there can be little, if any, significant organizational learning.

In most health care organizations, for example, suggestion systems are considered something of a bad joke; suggestion boxes are more often filled with gum wrappers than ideas for improvement. While we would acknowledge that an effective suggestion system requires effort to encourage and manage, other industries *have* made such programs the source of significant learning. At Toyota, for example, there are published estimates of more than 30 *implemented* suggestions per year per employee. How can this be? One factor often cited for this phenomenal success is that managers are empowered to *approve but not reject* any suggestion made. If a manager does not believe that implementation of at least a pilot effort is warranted, then the suggestion is automatically reviewed by the manager's boss. Think about this. How often would a department head at least try out a new idea if every rejected or neglected idea automatically landed on a vice president's desk? Too often, managers are placed in the position of having to defend every "yes" instead of having to justify every "no."

In too many organizations, open expression of conflict is perceived as either a form of noncompliance or, perhaps, the psychopathological consequence of unresolved hostility. At the risk of being framed as stubborn—like some patient who refuses to stop smoking—or, worse still, as crazy in the face of superior wisdom, many managers and employees alike seek the safe ground of silence, compliance, or private learning without public sharing. This aversion to conflict would seem to have at least some roots in the tradition of professional deference that physicians show each other at case conferences and morbidity and

Prescription for Action Strategies

- Establish a research and design function with a charter to go beyond the incrementalism of traditional continuous quality improvement into the exponential growth potential other industries have realized (for example, Nike, Microsoft, Disney) from *their* R&D efforts.
- Recognize, and occasionally reward, failed creative efforts to battle the culture—so common in health care—of treating imperfection as a source of eternal litigation, humiliation, or career termination.
- Health care leaders need to announce their own efforts to innovate, especially those that are not immediately fruitful. Your employees are listening.
- Seek disconfirming data and encourage open challenges to proposed decisions until such time as a decision is made.
- Incorporate the expectation of innovation and invention into performance reviews. Without systems that encourage innovation, few individuals will have the courage to strike out on their own.

mortality rounds. Most modern research on the source of creativity references the Greek god Janus of the two faces—meaning that without confrontation of opposing points of view, there is little chance that a new synthesis (that is, learning) will emerge to replace the old, safe, and obsolete ways of doing things.

Diagnostic Questions to Ask in Your Health Care Organization

- What procedures, practices, processes, and programs have other health care organizations copied from your health care organization?
- How are lessons learned from mistakes and failure actively shared in your health care organization?
- How often do managers at each level seek disconfirming data or opposing views prior to making a decision or initiating action?
- How many breakthrough innovations have been implemented as a result of your continuous quality improvement efforts?

CONCLUSION

While we have attempted to identify some of the more commonly manifested symptoms of misalignment in modern health care organizations, our experience also tells us that your health care organization undoubtedly has novel symptoms that impede momentum and create imbalance. The critical issue is to identify the gaps in alignment—in structure, information, rewards, people, learning systems, and work processes—that are actively *constraining* your health care organization from realizing its most critical goals.

While the medical literature is filled with case studies of spontaneous remission of symptoms and disease, the consequences of enabling random design to drive the future outcomes for your health care organization are too severe to relegate to the vicissitudes of chance. The intent of each of the following chapters is to provide practical approaches to closing the gaps of misalignment in ways that will enable your health care organization to achieve both balance and momentum in the service of patients, professionals, and performance.

3

Core Process Redesign (CPR) Aligning Process with Strategy and Results

WHY REDESIGN?

We need to redesign because of some very powerful external driving forces that are affecting the delivery of health care in the United States. Economic forces, especially prospective payment and managed care, are forcing changes in the delivery system. Capitalization will drive reduced resource utilization and tighter fiscal control. Diminished resources will dictate examination of the methods and outcomes of health care delivery.

Reduction in Medicare case volume and an increase in managed care case volume is a trend that will continue in the future. This trend will force us to focus on continually reducing costs while maintaining the quality of our services to remain a viable vendor. The redefined health care environment will have less emphasis on "sick care" and more emphasis on "health care"—*primary prevention*, including wellness, fitness, and occupational health. *Secondary prevention* will become a focus as well, emphasizing such things as home care, hospices, transition care, and assisted living, to name a few. Pressure to reduce both utilization and costs will continue to intensify and ventures external to the acute arena will require greater reserves.

While many health care organizations have developed strategies in response to these external forces, far fewer organizations—hospitals, health systems, group practices—have evolved internal alignment of core processes to link today's strategies with market and customer demand for measurable results. This alignment rarely occurs as a random function of hoped-for results. Alignment demands core process redesign. Otherwise, current gaps in alignment will drive both poor performance and inconsistent clinical outcomes. A few examples from health care organizations prior to their core process redesign efforts may illustrate the risk:

- A small specialty hospital in the Northeast had a traditional functional structure that drove resources to all clinical services in an almost democratic manner despite the reality that 60 percent of its revenue and 80 percent of its margin were derived from a single clinical service.
- A major medical group practice of over 500 physicians in the Midwest had a reward system that compensated physicians for tenure, specialty, and patient satisfaction, but did not pay for performance, nonclinical contributions to practice functioning, or efficient delivery of care.
- A major academic medical center in the Southeast maintained a state-of-the-art information system that most physicians and many managers found to be hostile to any but the most sophisticated users.
- A community hospital in the Midwest developed a "universal worker" model for the delivery of many support services, but made no investment in a learning system that might enable workers to make the transition from old, familiar jobs to new, more complex and demanding work.
- Another suburban community hospital initiated a significant reduction in force—including outplacement, retirement packages, and stress management classes—without consideration for the strain and demand on the surviving people who were expected to increase productivity to compensate for the reduced staff.
- A final example is that of a publicly funded city hospital in need of access to managed care contracts but with no work process for marketing to prospective payers and engaging them in business negotiations.

In each of these examples, the absence of core process redesign clearly constrained progress toward critical strategic objectives and increased the risk of less than optimal business and clinical results. There was simply too little *alignment* of strategy, process, and results to assure success.

LACK OF DESIGN IN HEALTH CARE SYSTEMS

Most health care processes were never *designed* in the first place—they evolved incrementally into their current state. This evolution was the result of adjustments to crises, provider demands, payer complaints, customer dissatisfaction, employer requirements, and employee frustration. This evolution was sometimes driven by decisions that focused on where the pain was versus a total process design. A specific response provided relief from one problem; another plan provided relief from another problem. We now begin to discover problems that are actually the unintended consequence of the earlier solutions. Pain is amplified rather than reduced. Finally, we have a process that is made up of both technological and human processes that are not aligned with each other. Processes that evolve piecemeal over many years resemble a patchwork quilt; processes that are pieced together over time tend to unravel because the threads that hold them in place start to fray and then unravel. Finally, we have a core process that is dysfunctional and costly to operate.

Most organizations do not take a systematic approach to large scale process design. Continuous quality improvement (CQI) as practiced in most health care organizations is not the answer. In too many organizations, CQI has failed to deliver significant clinical outcomes or business results. Since the CQI process itself was designed for incremental improvement and not rapid breakthroughs in performance, perhaps CQI has inadvertently become a technology in need of redesign.

CORE PROCESS REDESIGN

Core process redesign (CPR) is a team-based change technology that drives rapid, constructive improvement in how work is done in a health care organization to enhance patient care and business performance. Core process redesign is also a systematic methodology for improving what, where, and how work is done in an organization if the targeted work can pass the “test of why?” The “test of why?” asks two fundamental questions often neglected throughout the typical implementation of CQI:

1. Why does our strategic intent demand that this process exist in the first place?
2. Why do our critical customers demand that this process deliver extraordinary value?

CPR applies a systematic approach to exploring the methods by which people deliver on key customer needs. It is a structured process for self-developed, large-scale change. It is not a quick-fix approach, a passing fad, nor a fast and easy approach to downsizing. CPR is *not* reengineering by a new name.

Core process redesign supports work teams in their efforts to develop, test, and implement innovative, practical pathways that result in preferred outcomes for patients, providers, and payers in your market. CPR will enable your total organization—ancillary services, management functions, clinical services, strategic planning—to deliver the flow of value to your most critical customers. (See figure 3-1.)

"Why and when to redesign" is a common question health care leaders are asking. The answer depends upon whether incremental change or small improvements in functional departmental processes will achieve the improvement goals the organization is seeking. If incremental change or small process improvement will not achieve the organization's needs, then a full-scale redesign effort—CPR—should be undertaken.

Identification of the critical redesign opportunities is a task that senior management must undertake. The first step in this identification process is to utilize data. Senior management should engage in a thorough quantitative and qualitative analysis of opportunities through cost benchmarking, interviews, focus groups, and potential strategic requirements for change. But whenever redesign is initiated, it must be aligned with the organization's values, strategy, goals, and preferred clinical and business outcomes. Without such alignment, achieving market leadership becomes improbable; sustaining market leadership in a competitive environment becomes impossible.

FIGURE 3-1. Core Process Redesign

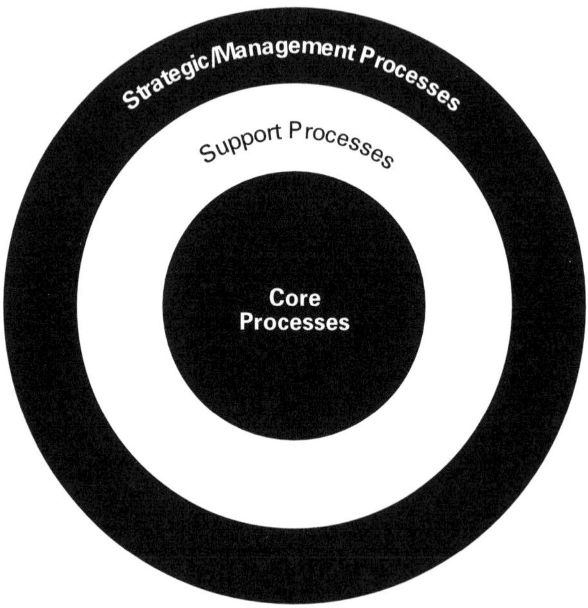

CORE PROCESS REDESIGN METHODOLOGY

Core process redesign engages teams in five phases:

1. Focus
2. Assessment
3. Negotiation
4. Redesign
5. Implementation

These five phases are discussed below and presented with case examples illustrating implementation of the core redesign process. (See figure 3-2.)

Phase 1: Focus

In this phase of CPR, the team leader forms the team with the advice of senior management and other key constituencies. The team then focuses on its charter, task, objectives, and overall mission. Spending the time to clearly define the intent and scope of the redesign effort is an excellent up-front investment. Redesign teams that have a clear and explicit charter are able to spend their time on the redesign rather than trying to figure out the intent of senior management.

FIGURE 3-2. A Core Process Redesign Pathway

Phase 1: Focus	**Phase 2: Assessment**	**Phase 3: Negotiation**	**Phase 4: Redesign**	**Phase 5: Implementation**
Form Team Focus Team • Mission • Scope • Objectives • Strategic ties • Measures	Map Process Assess Capabilities Assess and Validate Customer Needs	Identify Unmet Customer Needs Negotiate Valid Requirements Set Improvement Targets and Success Measures	ACT • Analyze • Conclude • Test	Analyze Implications Seek Approval Refine Monitor and Measure
Outcome: Establish the change imperative and guiding principles	*Outcome:* Understand the current business situation	*Outcome:* Define real requirements and gaps in performance	*Outcomes:* Develop the change plan Pilot testing Refinements	*Outcome:* Dramatically improved performance

Procurement Core Process Redesign Team

The mission of a procurement CPR team was to plan, record, and redesign the processes of selecting, receiving, storing, distributing, and paying for hospital products and/or services. The team was committed to enhanced customer service, preservation of core hospital values, and a savings target of $1,150,000. These measures of success were driven, in part, by analysis and recommendations provided by Changing Healthcare, Inc., and its strategic partner, the Healthcare Management Council, which provided the benchmark data used to set the savings target.

The team wanted to generate the cost savings in nonsalary and salary expenses (the latter as necessary) and streamline procurement operations through enhanced timeliness, efficiency, and customer focus. The scope of the team's work included reviewing and analyzing 14 areas and 24 different processes. The team focused on 4 key areas of redesign: materials management, hospital cost management committees, linen, and service contracts.

The team started with a clear objective, definite boundaries, and a savings target to achieve. This team started its first meeting on redesign of the process and not on designing a charter for itself. The charter was reviewed with senior management and modified when appropriate.

Identification of the critical redesign opportunities is a task that senior management must undertake. Senior management must engage in a thorough quantitative and qualitative analysis of opportunities through cost benchmarking, interviews, focus groups, and potential strategic requirement for change. The first step in this identification process is to utilize data to select the critical core processes for redesign. Then the chartering process can begin. Senior management must decide how many CPR teams it has resources to support concurrently. The next step is to develop clear and specific charters for each redesign team.

It should be emphasized that a clear charter from senior management is imperative if a redesign team is to get off to a fast and effective start. When the charter is not clear, the team can spend four to five meetings trying to figure out what senior management wanted them to do. Senior management should never charter a redesign team until they know exactly what they want the team to accomplish. Modifications to a charter can take place as the redesign team uncovers data that may support a modification or expansion of the scope of their work. Senior management must make a great effort to ensure that the redesign team understands the "why" of their formation and the scope of their work. Being clear about the real reason(s) for redesign greatly helps to focus a team from the outset.

Phase 2: Assessment

In this phase of the core process redesign, the team maps the real processes under study, assesses the process capabilities, and determines customer needs.

The biggest mistake that teams make in this phase is not interviewing all their customers, not probing for details, assuming they know what the customer wants, and dismissing some customer needs as complaints. Every customer need must be evaluated in the redesign. No customer-expressed need can be dismissed until it is properly evaluated and confirmed. Senior management, during team reviews, should question team leaders to ensure that they have done an adequate job of investigating all customer needs. The last thing a senior manager wants to hear in a final redesign team presentation is "No one ever asked me" from one of the customer groups.

Phase 3: Negotiation

In this phase of the redesign process, the team identifies unmet customer needs (performance gaps), negotiates valid process requirements with the customer, sets improvement targets for the process, and establishes success measures with the customer.

When evaluating a redesign proposal, senior management should ensure that the team has defined real requirements and gaps in perfor-

Patient Services Redesign Team

A patient services redesign team targeted the nursing, pharmacy, radiology, laboratory, medical records, and case management processes as the critical areas that affect patient services. The redesign team created flowcharts of all the current target areas and completed an activity analysis of each. An activity analysis is the measurement of a process's cycle time, cost, and quality. This analysis was accomplished through observation, interviews, and questionnaires.

The team also completed a customer needs assessment of each process they flowcharted through the use of surveys and interviews. These customer needs were analyzed and checked to determine their validity—were they really needed or simply long-held wishes for convenience? The outcome of this phase was the clear description of how the various processes currently function. The team also completed the plan for the satisfaction of customer needs in the future phases of redesign.

Home Health Agency Redesign Team

A home health agency redesign team identified unmet customer needs (performance gaps), negotiated valid process requirements with the customer, set improvement targets for the process, and established success measures with the customer.

The home health team performed the following tasks:

- They performed Process Performance Triage™ (a CPR tool), which prioritizes customer needs. This was performed for the referral, admissions, and support services.
- They reviewed performance as it related to existing systems.
- They reviewed open personnel requisitions for possible elimination of FTE positions.
- They analyzed the issue of employee turnover and developed a process to cut the turnover rate in half.

At the conclusion of the negotiation of the redesign process, the home health care redesign team was able to accomplish the following projects:

- They verified the strategic direction of the team's redesign effort, which was cycle-time improvement, cost reduction, and service enhancement.
- They defined and documented the admission, referral, and scheduling processes.
- They developed a model for cost management for the agency.
- They defined and documented a total revision of the scheduling and on-call system.
- They revised the jobs of the medical records employees and clerical staff to become clinical service assistants.

mance that is supported by data. Redesign teams must, in this phase, show how the redesign will make needed improvements and close performance gaps. The redesign team should also establish performance targets and success measures for the new process in their proposal. Senior management must closely examine these improvements to feel comfortable that the problem set out to be solved has really been solved.

Phase 4: Redesign

This phase of the core process redesign is known by the acronym ACT. ACT stands for analyze, conclude, and test. The home health care redesign team used the Process Angiogram™ (a CPR tool), which is a graphic representation of the inefficiencies in a work process and helps to pinpoint trouble spots in a process. Each of the target processes used

Information Technology Redesign Team

An information technology redesign team prioritized the information technology needs into four segments: identified imperatives, identified high priorities, identified medium priorities, and identified low priorities. This prioritization helped the team focus the recommendations that they would make in their final report to senior management. After extensive analysis of all the data collected, the team decided that the information systems strategic direction should focus on addressing the immediate needs of the infrastructure and managed care, and on improving current systems while investigating strategies to begin addressing long-term needs.

the Process Angiogram™, and new flowcharts and maps were developed that either improved or changed the system. Each new map closed gaps and improved performance. The team then tested the new maps or work flows to determine the improvements in cycle time, cost, and quality that were gained.

The information technology governance group must be empowered to set direction and priorities, allocate and commit resources, and monitor information technology projects. This governance group must ensure that information systems (I/S) projects are consistent with evolving hospital business plans and balance the sometimes opposing needs for clinical, managed care, and financial systems. The governance group must evaluate major project proposals and determine organizational I/S priorities based on support for the hospital's strategic goals and business initiatives. The governance group must work with the I/S department to establish adequate funding levels for information technology infrastructure projects and other I/S projects. The governance group should also periodically review the performance of I/S relative to the I/S strategic plan and ensure that it is on track. If not, the two groups should develop action plans.

The Redesign Recommendations

- The team recommended an open information technology architecture.
- The team recommended that the existing I/S organization (part of it was in the finance department) be reorganized and expanded under a chief information officer (a new position). They also recommended that the I/S department be increased by nine new full-time employees. This recommendation underscored the past lack of adequate investment in resources and staff in the I/S function. These new positions would be focused

on network analysis, a user coordinator, help desk, and software education. These new positions would help support the new applications and network to be installed and improve customer support and satisfaction.

- The team recommended that senior management commit $12.9 million dollars of capital and operating costs over the next three fiscal years to implement the following I/S projects:
—Information technology (IT) infrastructure: $3.2 million
—Information systems (I/S) staffing: $450,000
—Clinical initiatives: $3.5 million
—Managed care initiatives: $1.7 million
—Financial/administrative initiatives: $2.5 million
—Capital replacement: $450,000
—10 percent contingency: $1.1 million

The team also presented a detailed implementation plan with corresponding timelines for the next three fiscal years. The team recommended a number of guiding information system principles and philosophies that must be adopted by the hospital to guide the future use of information technology. Some of the principles and philosophies are as follows:

- Customization of package systems will be allowed but discouraged.
- Hardware purchases will be driven primarily by the application selected.
- All I/S projects must have an appropriate level of user participation.
- All purchases of I/S technology must support open standards to promote connectivity with the overall system architecture.
- All hospital renovations and new construction must involve appropriate representation from I/S.
- The hospital will work with the affiliated network to ensure that maximum value is obtained from I/S investments and that a highly open system is developed.

Presenting the redesign proposal is one part of the redesign team's responsibility. The other part is to present a change plan, the "how" of the plan's implementation. The redesign proposal must show the results of a pilot test that verifies that the recommended changes will work. Real-world experiments can show that the concept works and will deliver the results required.

Senior management must ensure that the change plan is detailed enough that it shows a step-by-step approach to effecting redesign in the health care environment. The change plan must include not only what must be done (tasks), but how they are to be done (behaviors); the training required; the expected change over time; equipment needs, layout changes, staff changes, and the communication process to explain to all those involved what and how change is going to take place.

Phase 5: Implementation

Successful implementation of a redesign effort is a carefully analyzed and orchestrated process that takes into account the anticipated effects of proposed changes on the people and systems of the hospital. In particular, the redesign team must seek to define the most probable *unintended* consequences of change. Anticipating the implications of changing the work processes on such things as the employees' competencies, the information needed to get the work done, and the types of reward mechanisms needed to drive appropriate behavior can greatly reduce the risk of failure and minimize resistance to change during the implementation phase. Once a redesign team receives approval from senior management to proceed with the redesign, their next task is to communicate the redesign changes to the rest of the organization. They have to develop a thorough and informative communication plan that includes using written announcements by the executive director, staff meetings, town meetings, care team meetings, and one-on-one coaching sessions to deliver the message of change.

Communicating the change is an often overlooked step in any redesign effort. It would be so easy if we could just post the new flow process map on the bulletin board and then everyone would just start doing the new process. Unfortunately, this is a fantasy. Getting people in a redesigned process to operate in a new way takes careful communication as well as appropriate and timely support. Otherwise they will resist the proposed change. People feel comfortable in the current process and like the status quo. They have adjusted to the current process and feel some degree of control. People will change and adopt new ways of working when they clearly understand why the change is needed. A good communication plan for change must include why the change is needed and how the change will be implemented. In these days of great change in health care, communication is a key ingredient for integrating the "new way" into day-to-day work.

After approving a redesign proposal, senior management must set up a process to monitor the implementation and ongoing operation of the changed process. Redesign, done correctly, should produce dramatically improved performance. Senior management must hold the redesign architects, including themselves, responsible for delivering the

Prescription for Action Strategies

- Following a brief period of discussion, disclaimer, and data debate, effective redesign leaders must set nonnegotiable targets for quality, customer/patient satisfaction, cycle time, cost reduction, and/or revenue generation in CPR team charters.
- CPR team leaders should be carefully selected to drive innovation, commitment, and results. The owners and architects of existing processes are frequently unable to lead redesign efforts as a consequence of ego investments and the predictable embarrassment "tax" of discovering massive improvement possibilities in processes presumed to be well managed to date.
- Select only keepers as CPR team members. It is naive and dangerous to expect team members to redesign themselves out of a job.
- Provide the time and technology support that CPR team success will require by significantly reducing the burdens of daily work of all team members. If CPR team–related work is secondary to business as usual, the redesign of core processes will reflect business as usual, not innovation and transformation. (If you simply *cannot* protect the CPR time commitments of certain critical team members, then external consultants may be necessary to staff some parts of your CPR project.)
- If a vice president or other executive leader will be held accountable—or will have to approve of the final redesign—consider the wisdom of making the VP the team leader from the beginning. There is a saying in some organizations: "What interests my boss fascinates me." In most health care organizations, everyone watches how leaders allocate their time more than how they frame their words.

promised results. Too often senior management does not set up the appropriate review and monitoring mechanism to ensure that the approved change actually takes place. Ignoring the implementation phase and review process is a sure way to guarantee implementation failure. Too often leaders just assume that change will happen, and it does not. Everyone involved thought everyone else was responsible for change.

Senior management must ensure continuity from the redesign through the implementation phase. They can keep together the team that recommended the redesign, appoint the manager who will have responsibility for the new process, or charter a new team to have responsibility for the implementation phase. The implementation phase can take up to six or eight months to complete. Senior management should schedule regular review (every two weeks) to keep themselves apprised of the progress, problems and obstacles encountered, refinements that need to be made, and the projected gains that have been achieved.

CONCLUSION

Core process redesign (CPR) is a team-based methodology for improving what, where, and how work is done in your organization. It applies a systematic approach to exploring the methods by which people deliver on customer needs. CPR is a structured process for self-developed, large-scale change. It is not a quick-fix approach, a passing fad or program, downsizing, or very fast or easy.

Core process redesign engages teams in five phases: focus, assessment, negotiation, redesign, and implementation, which result in a redesign process. Once CPR is completed, the redesign team must prepare the organization for change—which is covered in chapter 4, Changing Health Care.

4

Changing Health Care You Must Try, Try, and Try . . .

We all naturally resist change. We feel comfortable with the status quo. We have adjusted to our current state, built our lives around it, and feel some degree of control. Our current view of reality allows us to make sense of the present and to plan for the future.

In the best of all possible worlds, people would be given the time and support they need to adjust to change at their own pace. Then they would be able to absorb the totality of the change and understand the positive and negative effects upon them personally and professionally. In addition, they would have a clear understanding of the future state and how they would fit in.

The reality of today's health care business dictates that if successful organizations want to stay successful, they and their employees must be able to change more quickly and more often than their competitors. Thus, organizations are constantly looking for new ways to increase the rate at which change can be made. Unfortunately, most organizations still try the "push it down your throat" approach to making change happen. Those that lead with this change model often are disillusioned at the resistance and rebellion it provokes. They sometimes feel betrayed and disillusioned by their coworkers. "It was really the right thing to do—why did they resist? What went wrong?"

Any change initiative must be led from the top down and the bottom up. The top-down approach provides the vision and creates the required structure. The bottom-up approach builds the critical mass, encourages participation, and generates support. Leading change is a shared responsibility of everyone in an organization. If the whole organization is not on board with the change effort, it will fail. Everyone must be pulling in the same direction to achieve the change initiative goals that have been set. In change management, everything in the organization must be open to scrutiny: basic operating assumptions are questioned; traditions are challenged; "sacred cows" are put out to pasture.

Change involves pain and loss. Many in health care "grew up" professionally with the security and stability of the fee-for-service health care model. Today's environment is so full of demands and uncertainties that there is a powerful nostalgia and yearning for the past. The major challenge that health care organizations now face is helping their people effectively manage this high level of change and uncertainty.

From our research and experience with organizations that have implemented successful change initiatives, we have found that change is nonlinear; there is often no clearly defined beginning or end. Change consists of a series of closer and closer approximations of increasingly ambitious goals, which are embraced by more and more members of the organization. For this reason, change can seem confusing and endless. Often, those involved in the change process feel as though there is no light at the end of the tunnel.

Effective change interweaves multiple improvement efforts. Organizational improvement includes increasing the focus on the customer, improving and managing work processes, and strengthening employee involvement. Success with one type of improvement often triggers the need for other types. Stalled-out change efforts can indicate not failure but rather the need to initiate or jump-start a change effort in another area. We understand today that there is no one "right answer," but that multiple ongoing efforts are required to achieve the change that organizations desire to make them competitive in the future.

Organizational change has an important personal dimension. The more profound the organizational change, the more important it is to create opportunities for people to adjust. Unless people can integrate change on a personal level, they can't sustain it organizationally.

Measurement is key to successful and sustainable change. The more an organization's goals can be quantified and progress toward these goals linked to individual performance, the more successful and long lasting change is likely to be.

EFFECTIVE CHANGE LEADERS

Effective change leaders frame the change in terms of objectives for the organization as a whole as well as for every individual. They create and foster an atmosphere where people are encouraged to test the new change and make their own recommendations. This open atmosphere encourages others to behave in a new and desired manner, yet allows for some dysfunctional behavior to occur while the change is taking root in the culture.

Effective change leaders guide the change effort through word and deed. They are the role models for the organization. Change leaders have the responsibility to establish compelling and legitimate reasons for the change, and at the same time acknowledge and identify potential sources of resistance. They display a constant dedication to making change a reality. They focus on results; they applaud success, analyze failure to determine root causes, and constantly encourage others to try again.

Change leaders interact with individuals and groups in the organization to explain the *who*, *what*, *when*, *where*, *why*, and *how* of the change. They use every opportunity to interact with others in order to promote the change, encourage challenges, and answer questions. Change leaders realize that many people are skeptical; while some are early adopters of change, others need convincing. They realize that there is a gap between their understanding of the need for change and that of the rest of the organization. They use every communication vehicle available to help close that gap.

In order to help close this change gap in an organization, change leaders must be able to create an environment where people involved in the change process can open themselves up to new ideas and concepts, challenge old assumptions, and overcome their resistance to change. Change leaders must provide tools, techniques, and laboratory settings to allow people to synthesize the new concepts and align themselves to the new way.

Successful change leaders recognize a number of truths about change and adjust their management approach accordingly. People have a saturation point for making change. Too much change leads to a level of counterproductive dysfunctionality. You must understand your organization's capacity for change and not exceed it.

Reaching Critical Mass

Change is a slow process. A change leader must work to obtain critical mass as quickly as possible, though the process may take longer than you'd like. The change leader must continually talk about change and its benefits. Enlisting people one at a time is the slow but sure way of building a critical mass of change agents. A critical mass of change agents that are in sync with the philosophy of the change initiative speeds up the deployment through the organization. Some people are early adopters. Others need to be convinced through success stories and the obvious buy-in of a critical mass of their peers.

Implementing change is not enough. Change needs to be sustained in order for it to take root in your culture. Successful change leaders continue to look for ways to sustain the change once the limelight is off by using performance requirements to keep the pressure on.

A change leader recognizes that he or she is always trying to balance order with chaos. It is a delicate balance to accomplish because employees desire order and stability, yet they must be ready to adapt to changing conditions quickly. To really implement change effectively, you need to be doing several things at the same time—always with an eye on balancing order and chaos.

As a change leader, you need to see the big picture. Make sure your change effort is aligned with your organization's business objectives. See the change in the context of what's going on in the outside environment, whether it's new competitors, changing customer demands, emerging technologies, or trends in government or the economy. Understand how these conditions will affect your efforts and how the change, in turn, might affect these environmental conditions.

A change leader needs to see the current situation not only from a "global perspective," but also from the local level as well. Getting out and talking to people—to the stakeholders—is critical for developing a thorough understanding of both the people and the processes involved in change. You need to hear their take on what's not working well and what needs to change. Develop an appreciation for their viewpoints and an understanding of why they see things the way they do.

Finally, understanding the current situation includes understanding your own feelings about being a change leader. Understanding the level of your own commitment—especially if the change initiative did not originate with you—is crucial. Get a clear idea of who (both inside and outside of the organization) will be supporting the change and who and what will be resisting the change. Before you put yourself in the middle of what could turn out to be a difficult situation, you need to take stock of your own priorities and commitments.

Drawing upon what you've learned from talking to others and from looking at the big picture, start developing a coherent plan. Because there is usually some disagreement on exactly what the change should look like, as change leader you will probably have to synthesize many different perspectives and come up with a tangible goal with broad appeal. Present that vision in clear, concrete terms that everyone can understand. As you describe the change to others, help them understand how it will affect them. Listen to the words others use to describe the change and try to use the phrases that make the change more meaningful to them.

Just as important, you must lay out a practical step-by-step plan for accomplishing the change. You must show what will be accomplished with each step and how results will be measured. Not only will this enhance the perception that your proposed change is a real possibility, it will justify the use of scarce resources to effect the change.

Implementing change always involves a trial period. Usually you have to try different approaches and strategies before you start getting results. During this phase, you need people who are willing to experiment with new ideas and techniques and who aren't discouraged by initial failures. Even if you could implement the change by yourself, you would need the help of others in sustaining that change. The old ways of doing things have a way of creeping back into practice if the change does not enjoy a broad base of support. As a change leader, you must continually involve more and more people along the way. This is how you build momentum until critical mass is achieved.

"TRY" CHANGE MODEL

To be successful in any organization, change management requires a metamorphosis in our concepts of leadership, management, employee involvement, organization of work, and resource utilization. If change managers could get people positively involved in the change process and channel the energy they expend *resisting* change into *experimenting* with it, they would move much faster in the adoption of new behaviors and ways of working together.

In an attempt to involve more people earlier in a constructive change process, we have developed the TRY Change model, as shown in figure 4-1. This model was developed as a tool to help change

FIGURE 4-1. TRY Change Model

Organizational and Personal Change Process

Initial Exposure To Change	Test ◄——► Recalibrate		Yes
• Challenge to personal change levers	• Negative gap ——►	Positive gap	• Postchange stability
• Fear	• Resistance ——►	Adjustment	• Acceptance
• Perceived loss greater than perceived gain	• Loss > Gain ——►	New gain > Old loss	• Generate new value
• Closed mind	• Receptive mind ——►	Open mind	• Experimental mind
• Destructive tension	• Exploratory tension ——►	Constructive tension	• Creative tension
No	**Maybe**		**Yes**

leaders and change agents understand why resistance to change is inevitable and to suggest some ways to reduce that resistance.

The minute we say the "change" word, people start to react; they display either a red, yellow, or green light to change, a no, maybe, or yes. Understanding how and why people react as they do is critical for developing effective management strategy. The TRY (test, recalibrate, yes) model highlights the personal side of the change process, which is often overlooked in the rush to implement another quick-fix program across the organization.

The TRY model shows that when one is initially exposed to change, it is common to feel fear. In any change situation we may fear that the perceived loss is going to be greater than any gain we might experience. The fear of loss tends to make us close our minds to any positive rationale for change and even to act in a way that will block or derail the change initiative.

When a change initiative is announced in a health care setting, it must be recognized that the change will affect each person differently. Each person (as well as the entire organization) will require an environment in which it is safe to react to and experiment with the proposed change. People need the opportunity to adjust to change before they can master the behavior that the change requires. The more profound the organizational change, the more important it is to create safe opportunities for people to adjust. Unless people can integrate change on a personal level, they can't sustain it professionally or organizationally.

We have found that people have four "change levers." Change levers are those features that can either block or support one's adjustment to

---

The chief of surgery for a large HMO was concerned that the need to reduce costs in her service would jeopardize quality of care and patient access, thereby violating her personal and professional beliefs and values. She worked with several trusted mentors to overcome her resistance to necessary change by developing new guidelines and processes for surgical triage that balanced market reality with clinical and human priorities.

A hospital chief financial officer felt threatened by plans to move to an "open books" management style designed to increase staff understanding and support of proposed practice and staffing changes. The CFO worried that he lacked the professional skills to present the fiscal data adequately, and he feared that he would lose some of his organizational prestige and control if he was no longer the "guardian of the books." He managed this change challenge by participating in finance seminars to upgrade his skills, and he worked with the chief executive officer to develop a new identity as "teacher of the books" that supported his beliefs and values about education and empowerment.

external change. The TRY model classifies these change levers as Beliefs (what I think is true), Values (what I think is good), Behaviors (how I do things), and Skills (my talents and abilities). Each of these change levers reacts differently to change at three levels: personal, professional, and organizational. The levers change at different speeds depending upon which levels are most challenged.

Personal change is the result of many small adjustments to these change levers. Change occurs through many incremental adjustments to our individual beliefs, skills, values, and behaviors. Over time the summation across an organization of these incremental individual adjustments produces real change for an organization. Change is not a process that can be forced or rushed en masse, but rather must be nurtured at a rate that is appropriate for each individual involved, as well as for the organization as a whole. As change leaders, it is our obligation to explain to everyone the realities of the situation and to set the pace that balances individual and organizational needs with market and business realities.

MANAGING HEALTH CARE CHANGE WITH THE TRY MODEL

Initially, those affected by change perceive a "negative gap." They feel they are behind at the start: "How can I change to that? I am not capable." This is one of the reasons why people resist. It is not the change they are resisting; it is the fear of not being able to do something new. People resist change unless they have adequate opportunity to adjust to it. People need to **test** change in a safe environment in which they can question without fear of retribution, influence elements of the change, initiate trials and experimentation with the new situation, and evaluate and manage the costs and benefits of change in an objective manner.

Once people are through the testing phase they need to **recalibrate.** They need to adjust their behavior as well as the change plan itself. They need to believe that the change they have made is really correct and valuable for themselves and the organization. They must feel that they have gained by this process in order to reinforce the change. If this recalibration phase is not successful, then people must go back and test. This can be a process that repeats itself a number of times until a critical mass of people feels a comfort level in each lever at each level. We must remember that this process is happening to each individual in the organization at different rates, places, and times.

An especially effective protocol for supporting ongoing testing and recalibration is by coaching. Coaching is based on the assumption that people benefit from stable relationships in which they can react to, adjust to, and manage important work events. Change coaching can occur in supervisor-employee dyads, peer-peer dyads or small groups, and intact work teams. Ideally, these coaching structures are continuous and officially sanctioned; that is, adequate time and resources are devoted to their effective operation. Cynicism occurs when coaching programs are grafted onto a condition of high change and work overload. We have seen the failure of many attempts to create good change management programs due to the fact that "patients come first." In other words, if time is not found and protected for processes that support change, all time will be consumed by patient care responsibilities and organization change efforts will fail.

Creating a *permanent* infrastructure (coaching/mentor relationships, supervision, strategy groups, and so on) that helps people to test and recalibrate before, during, and after each change cycle will be more effective than one created in the heat of a specific change campaign. Health care professionals will become cynical about the use of strategic planning retreats, coaching plans, and consultation programs if they are too closely tied to specific change episodes and then dropped. The resulting message: "These programs are part of *implementing* change rather than helping us to *manage* ongoing change effectively." Developing permanent structures that allow people to work individually and together to cope with change can support the development of creative tension ("What's next?") and an experimental (versus closed) mind-set.

Providing the clear and specific performance requirements that change will need is also a critical element in effective change management. Giving people specific result levels to shoot for serves a number of purposes. First, it helps to make change more understandable in terms of both individual and organizational performance expectations. Second, tracking results gives everyone a sense of progress and offers opportunities to celebrate as each milestone is reached. Third, developing specific performance requirements increases the motivation to

---

As a medical group expanded rapidly, its leaders decided to implement a centralized patient scheduling system that left its primary care physicians feeling a loss of control over important triage decisions as well as over the scheduling of their own workday. Several valued doctors resigned or threatened to do so; morale plummeted. By failing to explain the need for structural change in the patient flow process and by not creating a process whereby the medical staff could generate its own solutions to this change challenge, the leadership guaranteed massive resistance and loss of trust. After several months, management instituted a series of strategy groups charged with the development of an effective scheduling system.

What if some of our assumptions about driving change in organizational behavior are false? So what?

You will perhaps recall that in the preface to this book, we noted that "alas, books and models do not change behavior." Embedded in every chapter and book on organizational change are assumptions. What if our assumptions about changing are false? So what? What if *your* assumptions about changing are false?

Assuming that your current action strategies as a change leader too often seem insufficient to maintain balance and momentum in a rapidly changing health care environment, are there any practical prescriptions that just might dramatically improve your effectiveness as a change leader?

manage change effectively. Finally, measuring results tends to sustain change once the organization's attention is focused elsewhere. Clear expectations and benchmarks provide the grist for testing and recalibration activities and for the self-management of the change levers that can result in optimal adjustment to change.

The senior management team needs time to test and recalibrate; the assumption that leaders manage change better than their subordinates is usually incorrect. Unless leaders have an opportunity to adjust to change together and individually, they will lead in a fragmented fashion that will increase fear and resistance at large. Leaders need to learn what is driving the need for change (such as legislative change, risk management, public relations, payer demands, or medical knowledge) and to develop a satisfactory strategic and action plan to meet those challenges. They need to create time frames for their own adjustment, for organizationwide testing and recalibration, and for final implementation. They need to review the impact of proposed change on their beliefs, values, skills, and behavior. Only then will leaders be in a position to initiate constructive change coaching with the whole organization. When the change conversation moves out of senior leadership and into the mainstream, there should be a *preexisting* change coaching infrastructure that can buffer the fear and loss described in the TRY model. Only then can people move from resistance to experimentation to adjustment.

CONCLUSION

Change management is the process of continually renewing the organization's direction, structure, and capabilities to serve the ever-changing needs of the marketplace, the organization, and employees. Change management must happen rapidly today since the rate of change is greater than in any other time in business history. The marketplace and competitive field are changing overnight. Alliances and structures are changing rapidly. Everything in the organization is open to scrutiny. Basic operating assumptions are questioned; traditions are challenged; the cost of failure is greater than ever before; and the tension within the workforce is high and needs constant attention.

Prescriptions for Action Strategies for Health Care Change Leaders

1. Identify your unchallenged assumptions about personal and organizational change.
   - A change in behavior follows insight.
   - Your health care organization can be prepared for change.
   - Change leaders act to maintain stability in the face of chaos.
   - An effective change process requires extensive planning, resources, and time.
   - We all naturally resist change.
   - We cannot initiate more change until things get at least a little better.
   - More change efforts increase the probability of greater risk and long-term harm.
2. Reverse your *unchallenged* assumptions about personal and organizational change.
   - Insight is the result of a change in behavior.
   - People are uncomfortable with and exhausted by change.
   - People cannot be prepared for change.
   - Change leaders must promote instability to counter the persistent equilibrium of your health care organization.
   - Managing the consequences of any significant change effort is of more value than planning, resource investment, and time in initiating change in the first place.
   - We all embrace change daily to avoid the threat of stagnation and death.
   - Things will only deteriorate until you institute more change.
   - Not accelerating the rate of change is the greatest risk inside health care organizations today.
3. Create a personal and organizational behavior change action strategy based on your reversed assumptions.
   - How would you act differently in meetings with other leaders? followers?
   - What do you assume will be the consequences of your change action strategy as reflected in the behavior of others if you act on your new assumptions?
   - What assumptions about your current change action strategies are you unwilling to challenge?
4. Develop a change assumptions map for your leadership team reflecting both self- and group observations about each others' change assumptions as reflected in actual personal and organizational behavior.
   - How does your leadership team collude to prevent change?
   - What change assumptions are most defended? Why?
   - What is the cost and benefit to maintaining current change action strategies?

Health care organizations must prepare everyone for frequent change to ensure long-term growth and stability. They must provide clear change targets and goals and a culture that supports personal and shared coping with change and the reactions that change creates. Effective management of the factors that can block or drive optimal adjustment to change will be a critical determinant of each health care organization's success.

Once change is achieved and in place, the organization must continually reinforce the goals and objectives of change through an effective performance management system. Chapter 5, Enhancing Performance, discusses the ways to continually reinvent management to sustain the gains.

5

Enhancing Performance Reinventing Management to Sustain the Gains

Performance management aligns the daily work of individuals with an organization's general business goals. This alignment helps an organization to focus each individual employee on attending to and completing work in an order of importance and value to the organization. The purpose of this chapter is to present managers with the implementation tools and techniques that can help them squeeze the maximum benefit from the time they invest in the performance management process.

Employees perform best when they know and understand the rules and goals of the game. They must have the resources and skills they feel they need in order to accomplish these goals. It's also important that employees' contributions are recognized and that they know where they stand in relation to performance expectations. Employees should be kept informed about future plans so that they can prepare and avoid inconvenient surprises. Has your organization already implemented the elements? Which ones are missing? If your employees do not know where they stand in relation to your organization as a whole, then this misalignment must be costing you time, money, efficiencies, patients, and business.

UNDERSTANDING PERFORMANCE MANAGEMENT

Performance management is a three-phase process that repeats its cycle on an annual basis to align organization performance with its business goals. The three phases of performance management are

- The establishment of objectives
- The provision of feedback and coaching to employees
- The evaluation of employee performance

Effective performance management programs encourage employee participation during the establishment of performance objectives, provide performance feedback and coaching to employees on a regular basis, reward employees for their excellence, and set the stage for the organization's future agenda.

The performance management process described in this chapter is not like the ones performed at most companies—it's not something that happens just once a year either to reward or punish, and it isn't something you have to do for legal reasons. These points describe a punitive performance management process that pushes its employees with fear and fails to pull them with motivation. Such a performance management process guarantees failure. On the contrary, a successful performance management process is joyful, positive, empowering, and motivating, and it works through regular one-on-one communication between managers and their employees. It can help an organization to attain its corporate business goals by developing and retaining valuable employees—those who contribute to its success.

PHASE 1: ESTABLISHING OBJECTIVES

The first step in effective performance management consists of identifying desired performance standards, winning the employee's commitment to reaching these expectations, and developing a performance plan that clearly explains all terms—procedures, goals, dates, and other such items—of the review cycle.

You have options for the development of your own performance plan. You may want to include a number of the following items:

- Major roles and areas of responsibility
- Projects to be accomplished
- Special areas for development
- Skills and behaviors that are critical to job success
- Priority tasks

By communicating these items clearly—including working with employees to make sure they understand them and agree to them—you give your employees clear direction.

Gaining Commitment on the Performance Plan

When a mutual understanding and agreement on performance expectations is reached, both you and your employee will benefit: you will know that your employee is on the right track, and the employee will be motivated by a sense of personal involvement. Certain parts of the performance plan will be mandated by business conditions and others will be more negotiable, but all parts should feature give-and-take flexibility in areas such as resources and schedules. Generally speaking, the manager should determine the strategic goal, otherwise known as the "What Needs to Be Accomplished" element. The employee should get involved in the process of determining and implementing the methodology, otherwise known as the "How the Goal Is Achieved" element.

Setting Goals

A goal is a specific end result that one strives to reach. Goals should be *SMART:* specific, measurable, attainable, results oriented, and time bound. A specific goal is a clear statement of what is to be accomplished. A measurable goal features indicators to show what is to be performed. When a goal is attainable, it is realistic and not wishful. A goal qualifies as results oriented if changes, improvements, or output are evident; a goal qualifies as time bound if target dates for completion are established and maintained.

Two types of goals may be set with employees at the start of the performance management process. Job-related goals define specific business-related results to be accomplished, such as "Increase center's patient accessibility by 10 percent over the next six months." Performance-related goals address employees' specific developmental needs, such as "Improve organizational skills by August 1." Both types of goals must specify how the result will be measured.

Measuring Performance Results

Determining how results will be measured is a critical step that must be taken during the planning process. It is necessary to account for measures of completion (MOCs) so that managers and employees can distinguish the tasks they have completed from those tasks that remain, and so that they can recognize when they have in fact completed their ultimate goals.

A measurable goal features indicators to show what is to be performed. A goal that reads "Develop a system to track doctor accessibility" is not SMART, but "Develop a system to track doctor accessibility for each medical center by January 1" is SMART. But "The system should track doctor accessibility for each medical center by January 1 without an increase in staff or budget and with approval of the medical director" is an example of a goal equipped with a very good MOC.

A measure of completion should include all measures used to determine whether or not the goal has been met satisfactorily. Common indicators include time, decrease in cost, within budget, increase in productivity, no complaints, no turnover, approval of users, fewer full-time employees, input from customers and team, and less than x percent increase in errors. Other indicators include accessibility, referrals, patient satisfaction, lengths of stay, patient retention, cost control (per member, per month), quality assurance, and utilization.

For example, if an employee's goal is to "reduce patient data entry error rate to no more than one error per document by May 31," then a possible MOC for that goal could read: "Quarterly average patient data rate charts show no more than one error per document consistently for three quarters." If a manager's goal is to "increase the amount of career coaching I do with the people reporting to me by the year's end," then a possible MOC for that goal could read: "Professional development goals for each direct report were completed by the year's end. Progress reviews were held each quarter for each direct report by the year's end."

Performance Planning Options

As mentioned above, a range of targets are possible when setting performance goals. You may want to identify major areas of responsibility, projects to be accomplished, special areas for development, and special behaviors that are critical to job success and achievement of business goals.

Major areas of responsibility are those responsibilities that are absolutely necessary to accomplish the job. For example, a manager may consider the following to be major areas of responsibility:

- Staff development
- Revenue generation
- Budgetary and cost control
- Project management
- Planning and organization
- Quality improvement

An individual contributor may consider the following to be major areas:

- Administrative detail
- Customer relations
- Interdepartmental coordination
- Revenue generation
- Training others

- Rewriting code
- Project management
- Sales

Resources

Discussing the resources required to accomplish the goal or expectation is very important. You may want to write down what you and the employee agree to be the resources necessary to accomplish a goal. Resources necessary to accomplish a goal might include

- Budget
- People
- Supplies
- Training
- Time

For example, if an organization's goal is to "develop a fixed asset accounting system for the operations department by January 1," and the MOC is "fixed asset accounting system developed for the operations department by January 1 without an increase in staff or budget and with the approval of the operations department vice president," then the resources could be explained as "Programmer dedicated to the project from December 1 through December 21."

Constructing Objectives

In simple terms, a well-written goal or objective should begin with an action verb, state the subject of the action or change, be specific, identify measurable standards, and determine time frame and assign weighting.

First, begin with the action verb. Action verbs give direction to your objective. Action verbs that could be used include the following:

- To reduce
- To increase
- To decrease
- To improve
- To maintain
- To install

Second, state the subject of the action or change. Subjects that you may want to change include overtime hours, productivity, turnover, computer training, admissions, and overhead cost levels.

The third step is to specify the subject of the action or change. The subject "overtime hours" must be further specified to ensure that it clearly and precisely defines what must be changed. Therefore, when you say, "To reduce overtime hours . . . ," you must specifically answer among what group, where, how many, and what type.

Fourth, you must identify measurable standards. Standards are specific conditions that should exist when the job is done to satisfaction. Standards enable progress or level of accomplishment to be precisely monitored and measured. By adding standards, your objective becomes more precise. "To reduce overtime hours of the accounting department staff . . . " is an example of an objective without standards. An example of an objective with standards might continue: ". . . from the current level of 20 hours per week to no more than 10 hours per week . . ."

And finally, fifth, you should be careful to include time and weighting. Include expected completion or "target" dates in your objective action plans. Although every effort should be made to specify precise target dates (for example, by June 30), there may be occasions when only broad ranges can be specified, such as "during the third quarter."

In order to ensure that the appropriate amount of attention is afforded to the highest payoff objectives, the manager and employee should jointly rank each objective in order of importance. They should assign a percentage to each objective, and these percentages should reflect how critical or important a particular objective may be relative to the other objectives agreed to. If, for example, an objective should receive an impact of 80 percent, both manager and employee should allocate their time and resources accordingly.

Once you've implemented all five guidelines, you'll have all the elements necessary for creating a solid objective—such as "Reduce overtime hours of the nonexempt accounting department staff from a current level of 20 hours per week to no more than 10 hours per week by November 25. Communicate department financial goals to staff to understand concerns and to gain buy-in to change in hours . . ." with a weighting of 20 percent.

Measurement

It is often necessary to devise measurements of present levels in order to be able to estimate or calculate change from the current level. The most reliable measures are concrete and in the form of raw data—for example, dollars of sales, tons of output, number of home run hits. When raw data can't be used, an index or ratio is the next most accurate measure. This is a batting average, a percent, or a fraction of a ratio.

If neither of the above two methods can be used, a scale may be constructed. Such scales may be rated from 1 to 10, a nominal rating against a key of adjectives such as "excellent," "fair," and "poor" or a key that describes "better than" or "worse than" for some arbitrary scale.

Verbal scales are the least precise but can be extremely useful in identifying present levels and noting real change. Verbs such as "directs," "checks," and "reports" are indicative of actions to be taken. General descriptions are the least useful but still have value in establishing benchmarks of change. "A clear, cloudless fall day" is obviously not the same as "a cloudy, foggy, misty day," but the two descriptions could be used to describe conditions.

The measurement statement should be directed more toward results than toward activity. (Most activity may prove impossible to state in specific terms, whereas results of that activity can be specified.) In stating results sought or defining present levels, you should convert verbal and general descriptions into tangible scales, ratios, or raw measures. If you can't count it, measure it, or describe it, you probably don't know what you want and often can forget it as a goal.

Manager's Tip Sheet

Let us suppose that you and your employees do establish goals for your department, but that your program still isn't working as well as you'd like. Several common errors managers make when setting objectives contribute to a general failure of this sort.

First, ask yourself if you're setting too many objectives. When no attempt is made to assign priority to objectives and to conquer them in a respective order, the abundance of objectives may choke your workers. An employee can attend to only so many objectives.

Second, check if your work team is suffering from insufficient accountability. If you set objectives but fail to follow through, your employees will develop the impression that you were never serious about your objectives in the first place. Once you announce an objective, show your interest. Never set an objective that you are not prepared to follow through with.

Third, consider the idea that you might be too forgiving of your employees. When objectives are not achieved, don't simply forgive your employees—if you do, employees will learn to take you and your objectives less seriously. When you find that objectives have not been met, explore the sources of the problem. Perhaps the objectives were not realistic in the first place. Perhaps the performance of your employees was not adequate. Perhaps your work team was faced with extenuating circumstances. Whatever the reasons, you need to find out—and then correct them.

Sometimes, a work team suffers from conflicting priorities. In these cases, managers have imposed priorities that are important to themselves but not to their employees. For example, some managers insist that desks be cleared of all materials before employees leave for the night. The employees may think this requirement takes time away from truly productive work and they will tend to not take such objectives seriously.

Sometimes managers come up with "ego objectives": projects that seem important to them and would, if achieved, earn them prestige. But if employees recognize these motives and do not see how they themselves will benefit as well, they probably won't commit themselves to the objective.

Ask yourself if you're the type of manager who doesn't contribute all of your available managerial resources. If you have the time, knowledge, experience, or skill that could help employees achieve the objectives you've set together, be willing to contribute these resources. In addition, let your employees know that you are willing to contribute these resources. Otherwise, employees may feel exposed on the firing line. Their resentment and hesitation to risk themselves may hinder their achievement.

PHASE 2: PERFORMANCE COACHING

Performance coaching is the process of working toward the performance expectations established in the objectives. It involves gathering information and providing feedback in formal and informal meetings throughout the review cycle. In addition to a formal annual review, these meetings may include periodic progress reviews and a midcycle update. Performance coaching may also include making adjustments to the performance plan.

Gathering Information

Information regarding an employee's performance can be gathered from a number of sources, including the following:

- A manager's personal observation
- Input from customers, internal or external
- Input from bosses, peers, and subordinates of an employee
- The results of a survey
- Issues churned up in written reports
- Evidence from work samples
- Issues raised in correspondence
- Performance during critical events
- Points drawn in the employee's self-evaluation

You must exercise high confidentiality while drawing information from other individuals. You should explain the purpose behind your inquiries and the ways in which the information you gather will be used. In addition, you should make it clear to your sources that the identity of your sources will remain anonymous unless their permission is granted for other treatment. In most cases, such interviews should be conducted in person or over the telephone in accordance with preplanned questions. You should take notes during the discussion and store them in the employee's data file.

Employee Data File

All information regarding an employee's performance is stored in the individual employee's data file. This file serves as the reference for performance reviews. Employers must be careful, however, not to consider the recording of information in an employee's data file as a substitute for giving the employee feedback. Events should not be "saved up" for future performance reviews—for if employees aren't given immediate praise or advice, they may not continue their good work or improve their poor work immediately. Feedback, both positive and negative, must be immediate and specific to influence performance.

A manager should maintain an employee data file for each employee through each entire review cycle. The file should include brief notations describing events with dates, times, and other relevant information. While developing your data files, you should remember to record both positive and negative events. Employees should be aware of the facts that data files are being kept in their name and that they retain the right to access their own files at any time.

Progress Review Meetings

Progress review meetings are held to exchange information regarding progress toward expectations and to make adjustments to the performance plan. You should schedule a midcycle progress review meeting no longer than six months from the last evaluation. You may schedule more frequent progress reviews depending upon the needs of the employee and the complexity of the work to be completed. Quarterly progress reviews are a good idea for most employees.

Conducting the Progress Review Meeting Before the meeting, prepare yourself by gathering information from various sources on the employee's progress toward expectations. Then schedule an appointment with the employee: explain to the employee the purpose of the meeting and allow the employee plenty of time to prepare for a discussion of his or her progress toward the goals and expectations originally established in the performance plan and his or her suggestions for adjustments to the performance plan.

Start off the meeting by establishing mutual expectations for the midcycle progress review meeting. Next, you should review the employee's progress to date relative to the performance plan. Be sure to praise on-target or near-target performances and redirect performance that resulted in deviation from the performance plan. When appropriate, revise the performance plan—this includes necessary revisions to weighting, measures of completion, and resources. It's best to close this meeting by summarizing the discussion. Ask the employee to review the action plans you've generated. And, finally, establish a date for the next progress review—this way, you'll be working to ensure that your performance review process runs constant.

Giving Feedback

Some of the most important information we can give to others regarding their performance relates to results and behavior. Feedback can help others become more aware of what they do and how they do it. To give feedback to your employees in the proper manner, make sure to focus feedback on the situation or the behavior rather than on the personality. It is important that managers refer to what an employee does, rather than comment on what they imagine their employee is. When we talk in terms of "personality traits," we often discuss qualities that are difficult, if not impossible, to change. Focusing on the situation or the behavior relates the feedback to what is possible to change.

For example, when a manager tells an employee: "You're a very disorganized person," the employee understands that the manager has already made a judgment on a permanent situation—the employee's personality. Given this understanding, the employee realizes that he or she can do nothing to change such a situation. But if the manager tells the employee: "Your report is not organized the way we agreed it would be," the employee understands that the report is not in the appropriate format and that he or she must change that format—this is, indeed, a feasible task. Likewise, if a manager tells an employee, "You have a bad attitude," then the employee may feel hurt and resentful, and still won't have the benefit of useful advice. The manager stands a greater chance of motivating that employee if he or she can keep the employee's morale up and keep the employee's attention focused on the specific point of the problem—by saying something like "You were late three times in the past week."

In addition, managers should focus feedback on observations rather than on interpretations. Observations refer to what we can see or hear in the behavior of another person, while interpretations require conclusions that we make from what we see or hear. An observation often can be supported by evidence or testimony; interpretations exist solely in the mind of the interpreter—who is, in this scenario, the manager—and doubtful employees can easily shift the blame to the manager. For example, if a manager says, "You were late," then he or she can prove this fact to the employee by presenting a time card or by calling on the testimony of witnesses. If the manager, however, tells the employee: "You're letting your social life interfere with work," then the manager not only opens himself or herself up to the possibility of being incorrect but also, regardless of the verity of the statement, offers an idea that cannot be proven or supported. The employee then is free to think or say that the manager is making wrong or unfounded allegations.

Managers should discuss with their employees the purpose of giving the feedback. Employees will be more receptive to feedback if they understand its purpose. For example, a manager could approach an employee with a statement like "I'd like to discuss how your being late to work affects the department's productivity."

When giving feedback, managers must be timely and specific. Feedback is most effective when given immediately after a situation or event happens. The issues surrounding the situation will be fresh in the minds of the manager and the affected employees, and there will be less room for dispute. And timely feedback can draw upon more specific details. Also, the sooner an employee is set on the right track, the sooner he or she can begin to work effectively. For example, if a manager tells an employee, "You're late a lot," then the employee can argue the point or dismiss the claim altogether; if the manager instead says, "You have been late four times in the last two weeks," then the employee is automatically accountable to those specific events—which by the way can be, because they are clean observations, supported by evidence.

Managers should focus feedback on the amount of information the employee can use, rather than on the amount that he or she has to offer. By overloading an employee with feedback, managers may be reducing the possibility that the employee will receive and apply the feedback effectively.

As part of the feedback process, managers should allow employees to develop alternative methods for correcting the problematic situation or behavior. Afterward, managers can add their own ideas and decide a method from those generated. Remember that most people do not want to be told what to do. It is critical to let the other person take the lead in implementing solutions and action plans. You should offer specific suggestions and coaching, but only after the employee has identified his or her own alternatives. Focus on helping the employee to explore his or her own solutions.

In the interests of both compassion and effectiveness, managers should be sensitive to time and place in which they give feedback. Excellent feedback presented at an inappropriate time or place may do more harm than good. After all, if an employee is embarrassed, he or she will be unlikely to pay attention to the advice being given; if the employee is angered by the situation, then he or she may consciously choose to ignore the manager's point. Corrective feedback should be given in private. Positive feedback may be given in public if the situation is appropriate.

Corrective Action

In most situations, setting clear expectations and providing coaching and feedback will result in good job performance. However, you may find that some employees will continue to deviate from agreed-upon performance expectations or continue to behave in a way that interferes with his or her job performance. In such cases, you must take corrective action: confront the problem directly and take any action necessary to reverse the situation. Like all types of feedback, corrective action is most effective when it is administered immediately after the detection of a problem.

First, consider whether or not addressing the problem means confronting the employee. Are obstacles beyond the employee's control hindering his or her performance? That is, will the problem continue despite the employee's knowledge of performance and behavior expectations?

Second, ask yourself if you have caused the problem by failing to provide the employee the means and the understanding necessary to meet departmental expectations. Have you given the employee the resources necessary to do the job? Have you been rewarding the employee, inadvertently or mistakenly, for not meeting expectations? Conversely, have you been not rewarding the employee when he or she does meet expectations?

If you determine that the employee is responsible for his or her own failure to meet departmental expectations, then try to pinpoint the source of the problem before you address the employee. Ask yourself these questions:

- Does the employee know what is expected—and when and how?
- Have you provided enough training, coaching, and feedback to be sure the employee knows the particulars of his or her job expectations?
- Does the employee know which behaviors are acceptable and which are unacceptable? Remember, your silence is implied approval of whatever is happening.

- Does the employee know why he or she is doing the job?
- Does the employee know how expectations for his or her work fit into the bigger picture of the department's goals or even the organization's goals?

Most of these issues can be addressed through development of appropriate objectives as outlined above in phase 1.

PHASE 3: EVALUATING PERFORMANCE

Evaluating performance is the process of assessing how well the employee's performance matches expectations set forth in the performance plan. Performance evaluation also provides managers with an opportunity to identify performance trends, which is helpful for future planning. This process can be referred to as an appraisal, a review, or an evaluation.

While preparing for an evaluation, ask yourself these questions:

- What specific goals or expectations were established and announced to the employee, both originally and during the process of review?
- Did the employee meet those expectations for performance and behavior?
- Was the employee equipped with the resources necessary to perform his or her job?
- Did the employee have the necessary skills to perform his or her job?
- Did any factors out of the employee's control affect performance?
- How may you have helped or hindered the performance of the employee?

Writing the Evaluation

Prepare the written evaluation by drawing upon the information you collected in the employee's data file. You may use an official form provided by your organization's human resources department or edit the document to accommodate your department's specific needs. Be sure that all peer managers in your department are using a common format.

All evaluations, regardless of format, must be reviewed by human resources prior to your discussion with your employee. In addition, certain elements must be present in all evaluations. For instance, all evaluations must include an overall performance summary. Customer comments, status reports, work samples, correspondence, management comments, attendance records, management checklists, employee self-appraisals, and your own notes should be included in the summary. You are responsible for collecting and presenting these items in each evaluation.

Next, you should expound upon the summary. While writing your comments, you must be objective, honest, and balanced. To support your comments, draw on concrete and specific examples. Make sure the words you use in your commentary match the rating you intend to give the employee, and make sure the rating itself reflects the employee's year-round performance—avoid commenting from a year-end viewpoint.

You might find it helpful to have a peer review your appraisals for tone and language before you submit it to human resources. It can take up to four hours to write just one evaluation, so plan accordingly. Remember to keep this a confidential process—be sure to shut off your monitor and clear your desk of documents and disks when others have access to your office.

Next, you must rate the employee according to a fixed rating system. Your rating system should be consistent from year to year and from employee to employee—this way, your employees will be able to see how their performance relates to the goals of the whole organization over time and to the performances of other employees at all levels and locations of the organization. Another benefit of keeping a consistent rating system is its applicability as a fair indicator within your organization's compensation department in the case of distributing merit money.

According to the proposed rating system, to say that an employee has "far exceeded" expectations is a comment of honor. To be more specific, this rating means that an employee has far exceeded the agreed-upon objectives of his or her job in all areas of responsibility and that his or her performance and behavior were outstanding. To say that an employee has "exceeded" means that he or she has exceeded the agreed-upon objectives of his or her job in most areas of responsibility and that his or her performance and behavior were consistently above average.

To say that an employee has "successfully met" expectations is a comment of contentment. This rating means that the employee has successfully met the agreed-upon objectives of his or her job in most areas of responsibility and that his or her performance and behavior ranked about average in comparison to those of his or her peers. To say that an employee has "partially met" expectations means that he or she has partially met the agreed-upon objectives or his or her job in most areas of responsibility and that his or her performance and behavior were inconsistent.

Conduct the Appraisal Discussion

While planning and preparing for your appraisal discussion, remember to keep the meeting a priority appointment. Give your employees reasonable notice of the meeting date and then stick to the appointment yourself. Identify a private and quiet place in which you may conduct your appraisal discussion—one where you and your employee won't be overheard, interrupted, or distracted. Then during the meeting, do your part to keep that place quiet—hang a DO NOT DISTURB sign on your doorknob and turn off your telephone ringer and E-mail prompt, and do not answer calls of any type during the discussion.

Think about how many discussions you want to do in a day. Don't try to breeze through your whole team in a day. Allocate at least one hour per appraisal and leave enough time for the employee to talk—at least half the time allotted. To save valuable discussion time, familiarize yourself with your employee's data file and plan your participation ahead of time. In addition, give your employee a chance to read through the written documentation you plan to discuss during the meeting—either present the employee with the documentation before the meeting or allot time for the same review during the first few minutes of the meeting.

You must be careful to manage the meeting with a fine mix of diplomacy and conviction. Try to anticipate individual employees' reactions to their evaluations, and try to understand and respect differences between these reactions. While comforting the employee as much as possible, be sure that your message, words, and tone are consistent with the written document. Remember to allow time for the employee to reflect and respond, and pay close attention to your employee's comments. Acknowledge the commonalities between your evaluation and the employee's own perceptions, and try to bridge the differences. Then, when appropriate, conclude the discussion on a positive note.

The employee must sign the written documentation discussed during the meeting to verify his or her familiarity with the document and the fact that he or she has discussed the document during the meeting. The signature does not imply agreement with the contents. Some employees elect to write rebuttals at this time. They may do so, and providing the rebuttal is of responsible and professional business quality, it should be attached to and filed with the appraisal document.

The rebuttal process moves up the chain of management. When an employee elects to draft a rebuttal, you must enact the process by informing your boss and your human resources manager. Your boss should help you to develop a strategy for resolving the issue. The human resources manager can support both the manager and employee individually in a difficult situation by coaching, listening, and preparing each person for a follow-up meeting. Ratings rarely change; more often, managers respond to rebuttals by revising their comments.

CONCLUSION

The enhancing performance model detailed in this chapter was built upon three fundamentals: the establishment of objectives, the provision for feedback and coaching, and the evaluation of performance. These three fundamentals form the basis of an effective performance management process.

Enhancing performance is a performance management process that aligns the daily work of individuals with the organization's business goals. The performance management process shown in this chapter is designed to help management clearly define the goals and objectives they want accomplished to their employees. Once employees know what is expected and how it will be evaluated, they are then able to align and prioritize their work so it adds value to the organization. Employees perform best when they feel their work is adding real value to the organization.

Core process redesign (chapter 3), changing health care (chapter 4), and enhancing performance (chapter 5) are linked in a cycle that must constantly be repeated in an organization to continually drive out waste, develop new skills in the workforce, and keep everyone's work aligned with the goals of the organization. Organization survival is dependent upon efficient processes, a workforce that can change quickly, and alignment of daily work to serve the needs and desires of the organization's customers.

6

Health Work Maintaining Professional Balance and Effectiveness

To thrive in the twenty-first century, health care organizations will need to take excellent care of their *professionals* (practioners and leaders) as well as their patients. The following chapter is designed to serve health care organizations seeking to increase professional satisfaction, effectiveness, and commitment to success. Whether engaged in performance management, team or work redesign, or systemwide change efforts, health care organizations can strengthen their competitive advantage by making a sustained investment in the work/career quality of their professionals and leaders.

PROFESSIONAL REVIEW OF SYSTEMS (PROS)

When caring for their patients, health care professionals perform a thorough assessment and evaluation in order to arrive at a diagnosis of health versus dysfunction on which treatment interventions will be based. This section will present a model for a professional review of systems (PROS) for professionals; it covers the core quality/risk factors that drive work satisfaction and effectiveness.

The Health Professional

A number of personal factors have a demonstrable impact on work quality and effectiveness:

- Medical health
- Personal and work coping style
- Family, cultural, and economic resources

A Hispanic nurse working in the ER of an urban hospital had little time for herself, between the demands of her busy job and her young son, whom she was raising alone. In reviewing her work life, she recognized that her cultural tradition of "respecting authority" made it difficult to question the way she was treated by patients, colleagues, her ex-husband, and others in her life. An adequate examination of her health, coping style, and resource system helped her to recognize that she was depressed, overworked, undersupported, and silent. This led to a decision to increase her ability to set limits and ask for help.

Optimal professional self-management over time should include a periodic "checkup" of these factors, with intervention appropriate to the situation, as in the sidebar example. Given their diagnostic sophistication, it should be a simple matter for health care professionals to conduct this type of self-assessment as an important part of quality practice.

The Health Care Environment

Research on occupational health indicates that the workplace can be dangerous to your health. By evaluating and managing critical work environment factors such as safety, workload, control, and resources, work satisfaction and effectiveness can be enhanced. While personal health factors can often be managed independently, effective coping with work environment issues will often involve problem solving and negotiation on the job.

The Person-Work Interface

In addition to the personal and environmental work health issues outlined above, it is important to look at the degree of "fit" between health care professionals and the environment in which they work. Significant mismatch in personal values versus workplace culture or individual work style versus organizational expectations can result in deterioration of professional quality and effectiveness.

Selecting a Focus for Change

Once the PROS process clarifies which of the personal, work, and interface factors are interfering with professional quality and effectiveness, it is then useful to select the optimal focus for effective problem solving

A primary care physician in a group practice with a large Medicare clientele was "drowning in paperwork." She often stayed at the office three or four hours after seeing her last patient to catch up on documentation, which interfered with her music, sports, and other interests. She believed that the group practice had failed to invest in the support staff and technologies that would make work less onerous, and she presented several detailed improvement proposals to the practice partners, complete with comparative analysis of similar area group practices. In addition to the resulting improvements in the practice setting, she was able to cut back to working only four days a week in order to carve out time for her avocational pursuits.

and action planning. This can be done by ranking the following change scenarios in order of their estimated benefit-to-cost ratio:

- Change *nothing*; continue the status quo.
- Change your life outside of work.
- Change how you manage work.
- Change your work (role, tasks, schedule, workload, and so on).
- Change your job (where you work).
- Change your career (what kind of work you do).

After defining where changes will be made, health care professionals can decide what changes to make and how to make them.

PROFESSIONAL LIFE QUALITY MANAGEMENT (PLQM)

Most health care professionals will work in their chosen fields for four to five decades, making significant career transitions every 10 or 15 years. Therefore, professional life quality management (PLQM) is a marathon, not a sprint. Successful PLQM requires adequate training and health maintenance, knowledge of the course to be run (terrain, challenge points, location of the finish line), and a race strategy that addresses course dynamics, competition, and current conditions.

Compared to their investment in other life sectors (such as working, continuing education, financial management, parenting, or housework), most health care professionals admit that PLQM falls into the category of "important but not urgent" (just like the exercise, dietary, and other health behaviors we know we *should* pay more attention to). PLQM therefore tends to receive less resource allocation (time, effort, money) than activities perceived to be either urgent/important (crises, breathing) or urgent/unimportant (some percentage of paperwork, chores, deadlines).

Optimal PLQM involves devoting adequate resources to periodic work life self-assessment and intervention over the professional life span. After a health professional or organization has conducted an adequate diagnostic PROS, it is imperative to find a way to act on those findings to ensure satisfying *near-term gains* in professional life quality and effectiveness. Otherwise, the investment in the PROS process will be seen as generating few benefits, resulting in low motivation for further efforts and ultimately leading to professional self-neglect. Individuals and groups that are most successful in their PLQM efforts tend to demonstrate a number of critical operating traits; these traits can be learned through instruction and practice.

Effective Self-Managers

Individuals who are successful in professional quality management have the following qualities:

- They create a clear vision of desired goals and results.
- Their action steps toward goal attainment are small, clear, and attainable in the short term.
- They work within their sphere of influence.
- Their self-esteem is adequate to support the pursuit of a good work life.
- They anticipate obstacles to success and develop solutions to them.
- They continuously evaluate the benefit-to-cost ratio of change goals and strategies.
- They define skills and resources (people, information, things) needed for goal attainment.
- They set reasonable limits ("bottom line") that they don't violate.

Effective professionals remain actively engaged with what they can control and change, and they find ways to limit the negative impact of forces beyond their control. They make maximum use of their cerebral cortex for developing creative solutions to work challenges, and they manage to avoid the "dark side" of the career marathon (fight-or-flight reactions, loss of work/personal balance, "burnout").

Active Coping Strategies

Research on professional effectiveness indicates that there are specific skills that help people achieve their goals; these can be learned, practiced,

A talented surgeon in her fifties and her work coach conducted a PROS that clarified that her work life distress was driven by very specific personal (anxiety, shyness, perfectionism), workplace (safety, workload, resources), and person-work interface (interpersonal style conflicts, gender barriers) factors. She discovered that while she was highly effective when she was caring for her patients or her children, she rarely demonstrated the same skill when addressing her own work concerns. This recognition resulted in a marked improvement in her sense of focus and empowerment in coping with work and career issues. She found it most difficult to obtain resources, seek advice, negotiate, or set limits on the job because, as she put it, "surgeons are supposed to be tough and independent, and women surgeons need to be more so." With practice, she was able to expand her use of these critical active coping strategies, achieving good results.

and refined. Effective management of work challenges is supported by the use of active coping skills. These skills include the ability to

- Evaluate problems
- Set goals
- Develop action plans for goal achievement
- Obtain necessary resources
- Communicate with others

Individuals who make use of these active coping strategies are in general more effective and satisfied than those who do not.

Energy Conservation Strategies

When running a marathon, athletes need to know how to pace themselves and even to slow down at times. Runners who try to maintain a "killing pace" over the entire course often end up killing only their own chances of success. Talented health care professionals can often be very strong in their active coping skills, but over time or when faced with situations that don't yield to their efforts to change them, they may experience increasing anger and helplessness. Energy conservation skills can help high-performance professionals to maintain a winning pace without burning up or breaking down. These include

- Relaxation
- Looking for the positive side of things
- Maintaining a sense of humor
- Taking the long view

A neurologist in his forties sought work life consultation due to disappointment about his failure to be promoted to department head at his hospital. He explained that while he was widely respected for his research and clinical prowess, he was consistently described by students and colleagues as "angry, critical, and controlling." He was told that in the current health care environment, department heads now needed to be leaders who could motivate and mentor people; these were not viewed as his strengths. Since medical school and residency, he had prided himself on his ability to "work harder and be smarter than anyone," and he viewed this as his strategy for success. In the process he had become alienated from his family, suffered from symptoms that his primary care physician attributed to stress, and now had lost the prize he had worked so hard to attain. He decided to conduct an experiment, telling himself: "Let's see if I can learn to work smarter instead of harder." He was pleased to find that his quality of life improved significantly within six months of learning to be more patient and take the long view ("I keep telling myself that people at the end of life don't wish they'd spent more time at the office!"). He continued to be ambitious and productive but with less of an "edge."

Fight or Flight

Professionals who fail to maintain a balance between active coping and energy conservation strategies in their PLQM efforts are vulnerable to sliding into the "dark side" of coping. When a person is unable to find adaptive creative ways of handling important life situations, there is a tendency to resort to more crude fight or flight strategies such as avoiding problems, fighting with or withdrawing from people, and giving up on having a better work life.

Fighting results in conflicts and alienation with the very people upon whom one's work life quality and effectiveness depend. Excessive use of flight or withdrawal moves one away from the people and tasks required for solving problems and can result in a sense of isolation and futility. The development of active coping and energy conservation skills can help to restore balance and effectiveness.

Creative Problem Solving for PLQM

One of the greatest obstacles to effective PLQM is cognitive paralysis, as in "I just can't think of anything I can do to make things better." The absence of promising choices or solutions to work problems is a major contributor to deterioration of work life quality and effectiveness; even the brightest and most capable professionals can occasionally find

A medical social worker was very dissatisfied with her job in a busy community hospital. After several attempts to improve the situation she concluded: "I can't do anything to make it better here, and I can't afford to leave." Over time, she noticed that she was becoming more short-tempered at work and home, had trouble falling asleep, and was increasing her use of alcohol. These symptoms resolved rapidly when she developed and implemented a PLQM program with an adequate dosage of active coping (action planning for work improvement) and energy conservation (regular exercise, more play) strategies.

themselves in that predicament. Strategies that allow one to generate positive goals, choices, and solutions can be a major contributor to work life improvement.

When we know what we don't know, it is a relatively simple matter to close those gaps by obtaining the relevant information by self-directed study, seeking advice, and formal learning or training. When we don't know what we don't know, it is impossible to close the gap independently; in these situations it is worthwhile to seek some form of coaching or mentoring. The information gaps that block most health care professionals are caused by their difficulty in accessing the knowledge, insights, and creativity they in fact possess; that is, they don't know what they know. Chronic work strain is known to interfere with higher-level cortical functions such as creative problem solving, and this can produce a negative work spiral. Fortunately, a number of learnable strategies (brainstorming, visualization, and right-brain techniques, to name a few) can rapidly increase one's ability to generate promising pathways toward work life improvement. Armed with new insights and options, health care professionals can move forward with action planning for work life improvement.

A third-year resident was struggling with the strain and exhaustion of training and was having increasing difficulty in finding any meaning in his work. He was actively fantasizing of abandoning his medical career, despite considerable talent and promise in the field. Having little discretion or control over much of his work life, he tried to imagine how certain religious and military figures he admired would handle a similar challenge. He was able to rekindle the values of duty, honor, and sacrifice that had initially attracted him to medicine and to see his work as a battle against disease. He also spent more time imagining how good he would feel helping patients in developing countries after residency as part of his medical ministry.

Effective Work Task Management

A recurring theme in health care is "too much work and too little time." Physicians and other health care professionals learn during training to work long hours and put the patient first—and to tolerate the personal and family costs of doing so. Given the increasing competition and cost containment in health care, there is little reason to believe that demands to do more with less will abate. And yet the negative impact of a workload that is perceived as chronically excessive is well known.

While generic "time management" programs can be useful, they often fail to recognize that problems with timely work completion can be driven by a wide variety of factors. Continuing with the model of diagnosis (PROS) leading to intervention (PLQM), the next step is to evaluate a range of possible etiologies for difficulty completing work within a reasonable time frame. These include procrastination, perfectionism, performance anxiety, lack of assertiveness, and inadequate control or resources.

After pinpointing the primary obstacles to a manageable workload, health care professionals can consider a range of strategies designed to improve work proficiency:

- Prioritizing
- Automating
- Disposing
- Learning and skills acquisition

CONCLUSION

The health of the nation depends on the health of the professionals who care for it. The limited costs of investing in their work life quality and effectiveness can generate an impressive return, even in times of competition and consolidation. As health care organizations face the

---

A talented physician was promoted at midcareer to a leadership position and after six months found that she was working harder and experiencing less satisfaction in her job. Her responsibilities for the oversight of other professionals as well as various quality and financial targets were creating an unmanageable workload overflow. She decided to decrease her medical practice and dedicate that time to improving her data, finance, and human management skills, and she sought out a seasoned physician leader for an ongoing mentor relationship.

challenges of practice and business in the twenty-first century, they might benefit from heeding the old adage "to heal thyself."

This chapter reviews what we know about healthy work. It can be used as a diagnostic (PROS) and intervention (PLQM) protocol for health professionals and organizations as they strive to manage the changing demands of the health care environment. The best professional self-management practices include

- Defining key personal, workplace, and interface obstacles to professional quality and effectiveness
- Choosing the change scenario(s) with the best benefit-to-cost ratio
- Developing an action plan with specific change goals, steps, and strategies for improvement; modeling the features of effective self-managers as professional development campaigns are developed and implemented
- Maximizing use of both active coping and energy conservation strategies while minimizing fight or flight and withdrawal
- Evaluating causes of workload problems and developing appropriate interventions
- Using creative problem-solving strategies to generate and refine choices, goals, and strategies over time

Epilogue: Not Just *Another Business*

MARKET DRIVEN TO WHAT PURPOSE?

Purpose tells us why we are doing something. Without clear purpose there can be little alignment of the action strategies prescribed at the end of each chapter. Purpose is both the reason and target for any strategy. So what is the *purpose* of health care? And is the purpose *different* than the traditional purpose of business to provide a good financial return on investment? Is health care really about a mission beyond margin? Is it about patients, healing, and the health of your community? If health care and business have divergent purposes, can they be truly integrated without irreparable damage to the best of both health care and business? Or is health care really *just* another business?

WHY HEALTH CARE?

Recently we have visited senior leaders of health care organizations—clients, friends, mentors, a former student, and doctors in many roles. Our selection criteria for the people with whom to have these particular conversations were broad and simple: They needed to have a good heart, a sharp mind, at least 25 years of experience leading health care at every level, and an abiding passion for changing health care for the better. We hoped to hear of an emerging alignment of purpose to drive closure of the many gaps outlined in this book. Without such alignment of purpose, the *why* of changing health care is missing in any action strategy. It seemed time to talk with leaders about the *why* that would continue to infuse the prescriptions for the *what* and the *how* in the body of this book.

Our intent had been to listen to the voices of these leaders and to distill their commentary into a brief epilogue of balance and momentum emerging from more than a decade of escalating chaos. Even with this anticipation in our listening, that is not what we have heard.

The complexity of achieving alignment in health care organizations in the next few years is clearly a daunting enterprise for each of the health care leaders we engaged in these critical conversations.[1] The candor and confidential musings of many leaders suggest that at least four critical conversations must occur on a continuing basis if we are to achieve alignment of purpose, strategy, core processes, and outcomes in the next decade in your health care organizations and in all of our communities.

Critical Conversation 1: Target Populations—Customers and Patients

The very word *patients* is spoken only sparingly—and sometimes not at all—in conversations with health care leaders. When asked, each leader confirmed the primacy of the patient as an assumed constant in the health care equations. But the conversation usually flowed toward *customers* and their variants—consumers, members, practitioners, constituents—except when speaking to leaders trained as physicians or nurses 15 to 40 years ago. In the '60s, '70s, and '80s, caring for patients seemed the common purpose of health care organizations—primarily hospitals and physician offices. And physicians were the undeniable customers of hospitals because they admitted patients and brought in revenue. Our purpose was clear. Now, patient care is but one of many purposes. Compared to decades past, there are other, competitive, and often triumphing purposes driving health care services today.

- In an hour-long presentation of key strategies to the board of trustees of a major statewide integrated health system, the presenting CEO never mentioned the word *patient* or the word *quality*. And in the subsequent discussion, neither word was used by any trustee of this billion-dollar health care enterprise. *Who is the target population?*
- Until recently, a nationally known specialty hospital refused to initiate discussion of the requirements for inclusion in local managed care plans because admitting physicians did not consider such payers to be "legitimate" customers despite the thousands of patients they insured. *Who is the target population?*
- In many communities, physicians, payers, and hospitals are in direct competition with each other for reimbursement dollars through redundant ambulatory care services without *any* coherent discussion of the impact on patient care. *Who is the target population?*

No wonder the patient care purpose of health care has become either obscure, presumed, diluted, or neglected in the babble of com-

Prescriptions to Ignite Critical Conversations in Your Health Care Organization

- Since meeting the requirements of your target population defines any business, what is your business?
- How is the voice of your patients reflected in the development and implementation of organizational strategies?
- How well does your health care organization integrate the driving forces of traditional health care and traditional business?

peting voices for the attention of health care strategy. Many of the leaders interviewed expressed immense frustration with managing this competition. They also seemed hesitant to be too outspoken about the primacy of patient care lest they risk being seen as either politically naive or overly idealistic in their approach to leadership.

Critical Conversation 2: Process and Power—Doctors, Hierarchy, and Control

In many ways, doctors still retain primary responsibility for patient care, *but* organizations manage the fiscal control of health care. To put it bluntly, it sometimes seems to be health care integrity versus business accountability. Our conversations with health care leaders focused on the paradox of every leader's effort to control costs and quality without the authority to manage doctors' clinical (cost-driving) activities. We also discussed the parallel paradox of every doctor's effort to deliver humane, effective, and quality health care within a budget not of his or her own making.

- In a very large group practice, doctors are not allowed to schedule their own panel of patients but are held accountable for timely access and "member" satisfaction in an exclusive contract to provide care to their patients. In this same practice, leaders are unwilling (or unable) to require that physician employees provide service at night or on weekends despite obvious patient need and preference. *Where is the integrity and accountability?*
- As full-asset mergers and alternative strategic alliances multiply among health care organizations in an urban bastion of medical excellence, integration and consolidation of clinical service lines (such as cardiology, orthopedics, and gastroenterology)

Prescriptions to Ignite Critical Conversations in Your Health Care Organization

- How have practitioners in your community reduced the cost (including their profits) to match the sacrifices of your health care organization?
- How has your health care organization redesigned clinical support services to enable physicians to better meet the demands for efficiency in the managed care environment?
- How have practitioners in your community assumed greater business risk as the basis for continuing entrepreneurial autonomy?

are stalled by the too-frequent insistence upon *local* delivery of complex, expensive procedures by physicians who sometimes seem more interested in personal convenience than systemwide organizational cost containment. *Where is the integrity and accountability?*

- Physicians and other practitioners plan to unionize to protect jobs and income while whole specialties resist reductions and relocations despite growing disparities between overserved and underserved populations. Practitioners everywhere decry the first net reduction in income in a century *and* adamantly resist any sharing of downside economic risk that is the bottom line of every other business enterprise. *Where is the integrity and accountability?*

What other industry grants privilege, protection from economic risk, prerogative, and profit as the perquisites of professional membership? It is only fair to acknowledge that few professionals must face the constant threat of malpractice and the burden of daily life and death decision making that physicians must embrace as a condition of work. However, in nations as varied as Spain, Norway, Kuwait, and Indonesia, health care is *not* an entrepreneurial enterprise and physician compensation is only 20 to 40 percent of physician income in the United States. Several of the leaders expressed the concern that the failure of the physician, surgeon, and management communities to balance patient interest with organizational efficiency is a root cause of massive excessive costs and redundant services.

Critical Conversation 3: Professional Commitment—Teaching, Research, and Service

A condition of forming a guild in the sixteenth century was a commitment to provide service without charge—*pro bono*—to the community.

These guilds are the legitimate ancestors of today's professions. The health care guilds of physicians, nurses, nurse practitioners, physician assistants, surgeons, psychologists, social workers, and therapists of every discipline abound in Boston and beyond. Everyone seems dedicated to expanding their guild while collaborating to constrain the next professional caste from rising beyond their roots. What is the cost of this proliferation? How is the purpose of health care or business served by such protection of disciplinary turf?

In health care, academic medical centers are often at the heart of this conflict of professional protectionism and public service. For many faculty of every discipline in teaching hospitals, seeing patients and supervising interns is secondary to grant applications, research, and publishing. How are patients and apprenticeships served by coming in third (after administration and research) in the minds of so many chiefs, professors, and directors of major medical centers? And how are the value and integrity of professional development to be assured if health care can no longer pay for supervision and teaching?

- Medical centers with significant medical school affiliations have built world-class reputations by funding academic/clinical superstars (and super clinical services) out of generous research grants and surplus operating revenues of days gone by. As Medicare reimbursement is cut back, government support for postgraduate medical education is slashed, and funding for research becomes scarce, contracts made in better times are binding hospital management to pay for work that cannot be billed to payers or charged to grants. And now, some of those same superstars are acting like "free agents" without any institutional loyalty. *Is this self-interest or service to the community?*
- Nurses across the Northeast (and elsewhere) threaten work stoppages and block the transfer of job tasks (for example, changing beds, transporting patients, drawing blood) to other, less cost-intensive, multifunctional workers. While their proclamation is usually to preserve patient care, the purpose often seems to be to preserve jobs. *Is this self-interest or service to the community?*
- The psychiatric guild (and AMA lobby) has spent the last 50 years attempting (and failing) to constrain the practice of psychologists despite the demonstrations of professional competence. First, the effort was to confine psychologist to the role of testing without the right to engage in psychotherapy. More recently, the guild (with an assist from the Joint Commission) attempted to deny psychologists staff privileges. Now, the effort is to deny limited prescription privileges without regard for the extraordinary preparation of professional psychologists everywhere.[2] *Is this self-interest or service to the community?*

Prescriptions to Ignite Critical Conversations in Your Health Care Organization

- How is the value of work that does not generate revenue measured?
- How does your health care organization distinguish and reward task-related job competencies from the politics of professional protectionism?
- What are you doing on a pro bono basis to serve the health of your community?

Critical Conversation 4: Accountability—Communities, Boards, and Stakeholders

While we all hope our personal physicians prescribe treatment based on a detailed assessment of our individual symptoms, health care as a system is simply too complex to be custom designed for every patient and every patient episode. Systems and organizations are designed to satisfy as many of the generic requirements of their target populations—in health care's case, patients, practitioners, and payers—as possible. An underlying theme of many of our critical conversations with health care leaders revolved around the accountability for, and ownership of, financial assets and patient care delivery systems. In other words, health care leaders (and many others) are asking, *Who owns health care?*

These conversations proved to be especially critical because organizations across all industries in a truly market-driven (that is, business model) economy tend to focus on pleasing (that is, being accountable to) their owners. This is how business tends to survive, grow, and sometimes thrive in every other industry already. Once upon a time the idea of a nonprofit provided a vague, if consistent, answer to *Who owns health care?* No more. HCA, Wall Street, Merck, Premier, IPOs, PPOs, PHOs, Blue Cross/Blue Shield, and regional and national managed care conglomerates too numerous to mention have made *nonprofit* a misnomer at best and a deceptive charade at worst.

- In one mid-Atlantic state, the major insurer (with over 70 percent of the market) refuses to negotiate with the many new merging health care systems, insisting on negotiating with individual hospitals to maintain its leverage in setting rates. *Who owns health care?*
- A large national health plan contracting with medical groups totaling more than 10,000 physicians owns all of the assets (that is, hospitals, clinics, technology) developed from income

generated by physicians for more than 40 years. The physicians went to court to claim a share of assets that now total more than $1 billion and lost. *Who owns health care?*

- A suburban community sells its nonprofit hospital to a for-profit company and then watches helplessly as services, costs, and reputation are downsized. Now the same hospital is once again up for sale. *Who owns health care?*
- A suburban community sells its nonprofit hospital to a for-profit company and then watches helplessly as services, costs, and reputation are downsized. *Who owns health care?*
- Physicians risk loss of license for prescribing cannabis for unremitting pain when other medications have proven ineffectual. Medications for the treatment of HIV are rationed based on cost while insurers attempt to screen out "at-risk" populations. Lungs and kidneys are distributed to renowned baseball players and to international highest bidders, despite proclamation of an equitable waiting list. *Who owns health care?*
- Parents of children with "preexisting conditions" live in terror of losing their jobs and their current health care coverage to the scourge of "reengineering." *Who owns health care?*

Many of those leaders interviewed reported a long-standing reluctance to support nationalized health care for fear of encountering still greater inequities, bureaucracy, and waste. All who were asked expressed dismay at the ineptitude of health care reform efforts in the early '90s. At least a few have been converted to the need for a single-payer system to establish accountability and to reduce the profit incentive in the current patient care delivery system. All seemed tired of the effort to please multiple masters without much alignment in expectations or much confidence in distinguishing ethical imperatives from economic stakeholders.

Prescriptions to Ignite Critical Conversations in Your Health Care Organization

- How does the board and senior management of your health care organization advocate for the ownership interests of those without corporate or professional lobbies?
- Who *really* owns your health care organization?
- When you take your child, your parent, or yourself for treatment of illness or injury, *who owns your health care?*

CONCLUSION

From our conversations with health care leaders, it is clear that the vital signs of economic self-interest are pulsing with vigor across the health care environment. And the daily demonstrations of true service and caring among people—practitioners, staff, management, professionals—offer the best evidence that health care is not (yet) *just* another business.

It is in the seeking of balance and alignment between self-interest and genuine service that the critical conversations of many health care leaders are ignited each day. As you innovate and implement action strategies in your health care organization, your first strategy must be to assure that the critical conversations about such uncomfortable, conflicted, and complex concerns continue. For it is only through the dialogue of such conversations that you can be assured that your purpose in changing health care is aligned with the patients we all, ultimately, are currently serving and whom we will all, ultimately, become.

References and Notes

1. A review of taped conversations suggests that direct quotes would be out of context, so we have elected to summarize without attribution in these final pages.

2. D. J. Anderson, S. A. Ragusea et al., "Staff Privileges and the Joint Commission," *Journal of Professional Psychology Practice* (February 1979).

Bibliography

Argyris, C. *Strategy, Change and Defensive Routines.* Boston: Pitman Publishing, 1985.

Burton, T., and J. Moran. *The Future Focused Organization.* New York: Prentice Hall, 1995.

Champy, J. *Reengineering Management.* New York: Harper Business, 1995.

Costin, H. *Management Development and Training.* Texas: The Dryden Press, 1996.

Finster, M., K. Muse, and G. Thornton. *A Comparison of Employee Suggestion Systems in Japan and the USA.* Madison: University of Wisconsin, 1988.

Gardner, J. *Self-Renewal: The Individual and the Innovative Society.* New York: Harper & Row, 1981.

Gerber, M. *The E Myth Revisited.* New York: Harper Business, 1995.

Gertz, D., and J. Baptista. *Grow to Be Great: Breaking the Downsizing Cycle.* New York: The Free Press, 1996.

Goldman, S., R. Nagel, and K. Preiss. *Agile Competitors and Virtual Organizations.* New York: Van Nostrand Reinhold, 1995.

Hammer, M., and J. Champy. *Reengineering the Corporation.* New York: Harper Business, 1993.

Handy, C., *The Age of Paradox.* Boston: Harvard Business School Press, 1995.

Hay Group, The. *People, Performance, and Pay.* New York: The Free Press, 1996.

Herzlinger, R. *Market Driven Health Care.* New York: Addison-Wesley Publishing Company, 1997.

Hoffherr, G., J. Moran, and G. Nadler. *Breakthrough Thinking.* New York: Prentice Hall, 1994.

Kanter, R. Moss. *The Change Masters.* New York: Touchstone, 1983.

Karasek, R., and T. Theorell. *Healthy Work: Stress, Productivity and the Reconstruction of Working Life.* New York: Basic Books, 1990.

Keita, G. P., and S. Sauter. *Work and Well-Being: An Agenda for the 1990s.* Washington D.C.: American Psychological Association, 1992.

Kotter, J. *The New Rules.* New York: The Free Press, 1995.

Labovitz, G., and V. Rosansky. *The Power of Alignment.* New York: John Wiley & Sons, 1997.

Leider, R. *Life Skills: Taking Charge of Your Personal and Professional Growth.* San Diego: Pfeiffer, 1994.

Maslach, C. "Stress, Burnout and Workaholism." In R. Kilberg, ed. *Professionals in Distress: Issues, Syndromes, and Solutions in Psychology.* Washington D.C.: American Psychological Association, 1986.

Micklethwait, J., and A. Wooldridge. *The Witch Doctors.* New York: Times Books, 1996.

Morton, M. S. S. *The Corporation of the 1990s.* New York: Oxford University Press, 1991.

Nadler, D., M. Gerstein, R. Shaw, and Associates. *Organizational Architecture.* San Francisco: Jossey-Bass, 1992.

Nadler, D., and J. Spencer. *Executive Teams.* San Francisco: Jossey-Bass, 1998.

Osburn, J., L. Moran, E. Musselwhite, and J. Zenger. *Self-Directed Work Teams.* Illinois: Irwin Professional Publishing, 1990.

Payne, R., and J. Firth-Cozens. *Stress in Health Professionals.* New York: John Wiley & Sons, 1987.

Pelletier, K. *Healthy People in Unhealthy Places: Stress and Fitness at Work.* New York: Delacoret, Delta & Doubleday, 1984.

Pines, A., and E. Aronson. *Career Burnout: Causes and Cures.* New York: The Free Press, 1988.

Quick J. *Preventive Stress Management in Organizations.* Washington, D.C.: American Psychological Association, 1997.

Senge, P., C. Roberts, R. Ross, B. Smith, and A. Kleiner. *The Fifth Discipline Fieldbook.* New York: Currency Doubleday, 1994.

Smith, D. *Taking Charge of Change.* New York: Addision-Wesley Publishing Company, 1996.

Stewart, T. *Intellectual Capital.* New York: Currency Doubleday, 1997.

Tzu, Sun. *The Art of War.* New York: Delacorte Press, 1983.

Wilder, D., and J. Weakland. *Rigor and Imagination: Essays from the Legacy of Gregory Bateson.* New York: Praeger Publishers, 1982.

Zairi, M. *Measuring Performance for Business Results.* New York: Chapman & Hall, 1994.

Index

Academic medical centers, 99
Accountability, 100–101
ACT, as phase of core process redesign, 50–53
Aetna Life and Casualty Company, 1
Alliances, 5
American Medical Association, 99
Anderson, Dan, 26
Assessment, as phase of core process design, 49
AT&T, 26

Baldrige, Malcolm, National Quality Award, 26
Blue Cross, 4, 5, 100
Blue Shield, 5, 100
Brown, Charlie, 26
Business
  dynamics of health care, 3–4
  versus caring as health care priority, 7–8

Caring versus business as health care priority, 7–8
Change coaching, 64
Change
  focus for, as part of professional review of systems, 86
  in the health care marketplace, 1–3, 4–10, 57–67
  leaders, 58–61
  mistakes made in decision-making during, 6
  TRY model of, 61–65
CIGNA HealthCare, 1, 2, 5
Community service. 98–100
Continuous quality improvement (CQI), 45
Control, need to, as mistake organizations make, 7
Coping strategies, 88–90
Core process redesign, 43–55
  definition of, 45
  methodology, 47
Creative problem solving, 90–91
Critical mass of change, reaching, 59–61
Customer service, failure to focus on, 8–9

Decision-making during change, mistakes made in, 6
Design
  architecture, 13–41
    critical areas of, 15
    elements of, 14–17
    symptoms of problems in, 17–40
  lack of in health care systems, 44–45
Disconnected structural elements, problem of, 27–29

Employee(s)
  data file, 77
  evaluating performance of, 81–83
  giving feedback to, 78–80
  performance, 76–77
  taking corrective action with, 80–81

Energy conservation strategies, 89–90
Evaluation, employee, 81–83
  conducting discussion of, 83
  writing the, 81–82

Family, work environment as, 36–38
Fight-or-flight strategies of coping, 90

General Motors, 26
Goals, 71
Group Health Association of Washington, D.C., 3
Group Health Cooperative of Puget Sound, 3

HCA (Hospital Corporation of America), 100
Health care environment, as part of professional review of systems, 86
Health care marketplace, changes in, 1–3
Health professional, as part of professional review of systems, 85–86
Healthsource, 2, 5
HMO Act of 1973, 3

Implementation, as phase of core process redesign, 53–54
Independent practice associations (IPAs), 3
Information
  addiction, problem of, 19
  as element of design architecture, 15
  gathering, on employee performance, 76–77

Joint Commission on the Accreditation of Healthcare Organizations, 28, 99

Kaiser Permanente, 3

Lagging indicators, 24
Leadership, lack of, 9–10
Leading indicators, 24
Learning systems
  as element of design architecture, 16

Management
  ignorance, problem of, 38–40
  versus doctors, 98–99
Market dynamics, 1–4
MCI, 26
Measurement, 74–75
  of performance results, 71
  recognizing and solving problems in, 21–25
Medicare and Medicaid
  case volume, 43
  and customer service, 9
  and HMOs, 4
MedPartners, 5
Merck, 100
Mergers, 6, 33
Metropolitan Life Insurance Company, 1, 5
Microsoft, 26
Misalignment, symptoms of, in organizational strategy, 17–40
Mistakes health care organizations make during change, 4–10

Negotiation, as phase of core process redesign, 49–50

Objectives
  constructing, 73–74
  establishing, in performance management, 70–76
Olsen, Jimmy, 26
Organizational design. <I>*See*<P> Design architecture

Patient
  as customer, 96–97
  resentment of restriction of choice, 5
People, as element of design architecture, 16
Performance coaching, 76–81
Performance management, 69–84
  establishing objectives in, 70–76
  planning options in, 72–73
  understanding, 69–70
Performance plan, 70–71
Person-work interface, as part of professional review of systems, 86
PhyCor, 5

Physicians
  organization of, 5
  versus management, 97–98
Pitfalls of organizations during change, 6–10
Planning, operational, 17–19
Politics of "who you know," 34–36
Premier Inc., 100
Process Angiogram™, 50
Process maps, 36
Professional commitment, 98–100
Professional life quality management (PLQM), 87–92
Professional review of systems (PROS), 85–87
Progress review meetings, 77–78
Prudential Insurance Company, 1, 4, 5

RAW Consulting and Development, 23
Resources, evaluating, 73
Rewards, as element of design architecture, 15
Rushing to solutions, problem of, 31–34

Sacred cows, 27, 58
Sprint, 26
Structure
  disconnected elements in corporate, 27–29
  as element of design architecture, 15

Target populations, 96–97
Task management, 92
Taylor, Frederick, 27
Toyota Motor Company, 39
Tradition, reliance on, 25–27
Travelers Insurance Company, 1, 4, 5
TRY change model, 61–65

Universal competence, myth of, 29–31
U.S. Healthcare, 5

Vision, lack of, 9–10

Waks, Rick, 23
Wallace Company, 26
Work environment as family, 36–38
Work process, as element of design architecture, 16